Daniel Boone

This inscription, which may have been made by Daniel on one of his later visits to Kentucky, was found on a tree that once stood in the Louisville area. The meaning of "Zois" remains a mystery.

Daniel Boone

Laurie Lawlor

illustrations by Bert Dodson

Albert Whitman & Company, Niles, Illinois

In memory of my grandfather
Lowell Dilts Thompson
(1889-1979)

Library of Congress Cataloging-in-Publication Data

Lawlor, Laurie.
 Daniel Boone/Laurie Lawlor: illustrated by Bert Dodson.
p. cm.
 Summary: Traces the life of the colonial pioneer, hunter, and
woodsman, from his youth in the Pennsylvania wilderness to his
adventures exploring the frontier, especially the "dark and bloody"
land called Kentucky.
 ISBN 0-8075-1462-4
 1. Boone, Daniel, 1734-1820—Juvenile literature. 2. Pioneers—
Kentucky—Biography—Juvenile literature. 3. Frontier and pioneer
life—Kentucky—Juvenile literature. 4. Kentucky—Biography—
Juvenile literature. [1. Boone, Daniel, 1734-1820. 2. Pioneers.
3. Frontier and pioneer life—Kentucky. 4. Kentucky—Biography.]
I. Title.
F454.B66L38 1989
976.9′02′0924—dc19
[B]
[92]   87-27373
                                                         CIP
                                                          AC

This book is set 12 on 16 point x 30 in English Times.

Text © 1989 by Laurie Lawlor
Illustrations © 1989 by Bert Dodson
Design by Gordon Stromberg
Published in 1989 by Albert Whitman & Company, Niles, Illinois
Published simultaneously in Canada by
General Publishing, Limited, Toronto
Printed in the United States of America. All rights reserved.
10 9 8 7 6 5 4 3 2

Contents

Introduction

"...I reckon I got to light out for the territory ahead
of the rest, because Aunt Sally she's going to adopt me
and sivilize me, and I can't stand it. I been there before..."

from *The Adventures of Huckleberry Finn* by Mark Twain

Americanfolk myths die hard. But
the fact is, Daniel Boone would *not* wish to be remembered as a rip-
roaring Indian fighter. Upon reading a particularly bloody account of
his life, he once complained, "This book represents me as a wonderful
man who killed a lot of Indians. I don't believe the one has much to
do with the other."

Throughout his life, Daniel was incapable of holding a grudge against
anyone, white or red, even in the face of terrible personal loss and tragedy.
He had neither the white-hot vengeance nor the furious "war spirit"
that seemed to possess so many early American explorers and settlers.
Perhaps it was because of the calm and clemency of his Quaker upbring-
ing. Perhaps it was because of his own compassionate nature.

Contrary to another popular bit of folklore, Daniel never wore a coon-
skin cap. His tastes were plainer. A comfortable old felt Quaker hat with
a broad rim kept the rain and sun out of his eyes on long hunts in the
wild forests of colonial Pennsylvania and later in the rugged hills of North
Carolina and "Cantuck."

Like the hats he wore, Daniel was not physically imposing. He was
not a giant, as he was sometimes portrayed in popular paintings and
stories. Daniel stood a stocky five foot, eight or nine inches tall. He

was broad-shouldered, barrel-chested, and weighed close to 175 pounds most of his life. Shawnee Chief Blackfish affectionately called him *Sheltowee* when he adopted him as his son. The name "Big Turtle" fit Daniel well.

He didn't wear fancy clothes or ride fast horses. Daniel's clothes were mostly homemade buckskin dyed black or tow cloth dyed brown for better camouflage in the forest. When he traveled, he usually walked. He seldom had enough money to own more than a packhorse.

Daniel was a quiet man who had a habit of whistling low between his teeth or singing softly to himself, perhaps because he spent so much time alone wandering and hunting. What motivated him was a desire for land, a love of the wilderness, and a hankering to explore, to find out what was just over the next mountain, beyond the next river.

He was uneducated. But when he spoke, people listened. They admired his remarkable courage and his go-ahead confidence that gave them hope to defy the odds and follow where he led. And when times were hard, as they often were in the frontier settlements, it was Daniel who drew people together and helped them pull through.

During his almost eighty-six years, Daniel saw America grow from a string of bickering English colonies clinging along the Atlantic seaboard to a unified country with its own government and laws, extending from the Atlantic coast to the Rocky Mountains.

He was more than just a legendary hero famous in his own time. He was a true leader. In the westward movement that pushed beyond that first big barrier called the Appalachian Mountains, Daniel Boone somehow convinced ordinary people to do something extraordinary—make the wilderness their home.

Chapter One

Seasons Spent Wandering

Night crept across the moonless summer sky. Soon the whole forest would be as black as the eye of a bear. An owl hooted. Where was Daniel? Sarah Boone stared hard past the crouching silhouette of scrub oak near their little log cabin and listened for her thirteen-year-old son's low whistle and the sound of the family cows approaching heavily through the underbrush.

She waited. And still there was no sign of Daniel or the herd on their way home for milking.

Daniel, born November 2, 1734, was her fourth son. Every summer since he was ten, he had come with her to take care of the cows and live in the small, rough-hewn house that his father, Squire Boone, had built near a cool spring. Daniel's job was herding and keeping track of strays on this twenty-five-acre piece of land. Sarah Boone's was milking and churning.

The butter she made was just as good as money, which was scarce on the Pennsylvania frontier. In the nearest village, Exeter, Daniel's family could trade pounds of the sweet, pale yellow stuff for a pair of boots, a chicken, or a bushel of seed corn. They could also make an exchange for Pennsylvania paper shillings and pounds to pay taxes to King George. Like the rest of the colonies, Pennsylvania was part of England, and

Daniel's father and his Quaker neighbors all considered themselves Englishmen.

While Daniel and his mother took care of milking and butter making all summer long, the rest of the family lived four miles away on a 147-acre farm. Daniel was the sixth in a family of eleven boys and girls. His oldest sister and brother were already married and had their own homes. The three others older than Daniel were grown up enough to help their father run the farm and take care of the little ones, who ranged in age from just a year old to nearly eleven. Everyone had his or her share of work to do. The children big enough to manage an ax helped gather, chop, and split wood to keep up the fire. Every morning the youngest gathered kindling in a basket. There were corn, tobacco, and vegetables to cultivate, pigs to slop, and forest to clear for new farmland. Squire Boone even had his own small blacksmith shop and five looms ready if a customer happened by in need of gun repair or a new bolt of broadcloth.

Daniel had every cause to be delighted when the dogwood blossomed and he and his mother herded their scrawny cattle through the woods to their summer pasture. Daniel didn't like farming or weaving or smithing or keeping an eye on pesky younger brothers and sisters.

He liked wandering. And herding cattle was as good excuse as any for wandering.

When Daniel was supposed to be tending cows, he often went exploring beyond his family's property through forests filled with bright moccasin flowers and blazing rhododendrons. Daniel roamed the laurel-covered hillsides and rich bottomlands near the lazy Schuylkill River. Inside hidden caves and sinkholes, he put his ear to the ground and listened to the strange rumblings of mysterious underground streams. During a high wind, the swaying top of a slim, fifty-foot-tall hickory was as wild a ride as any unbroken Indian pony. Daniel could hold on tight and yell and sing at the top of his lungs with no one around to say "Be quiet" or "Climb down before thee breaks thy neck."

The forest was Daniel's teacher. Always fascinated by animals, he

10

observed the ways of lazy box turtles, leopard toads, and five-lined skink lizards. He spied on busy otter and beaver. With the gun his father had given him, he silently tracked signs of deer and ruffled grouse in dense hemlock along stream banks. Like other boys his age, he practiced imitating the soft bleating of fawns to attract does and the hooting of owls and the gobbling of wild turkeys to bring birds closer.

There were all manner of things that the woods could provide. Daniel and his family were dependent on the seemingly endless forest for material to build their house, barns, and fences; to fuel their fire; to carve their pitchforks and gunstocks. Daniel learned where to hunt a slender hickory sapling to make his mother a corn-pounder sweep and where to find the best small crooked white oak to carve a sled runner. He learned which wood would bend, which would sink, which would float, which was strong enough to use for a splitting maul, and which was soft enough to carve into a trencher.[1]

There were plants in the forest that could cure snakebite and fever and others that could keep off ticks. Daniel came to recognize these and many more. He discovered where to find the sweetest serviceberries and blackberries and the finest hickory nuts, black walnuts, hazelnuts, and chestnuts. There were wild strawberries to be gathered on "bald knobs," or treeless hills along creeks in early spring; black haws on large bushes in sloughs after the first frost; and crab apples hidden sweet, golden, and fragrant under leaves when the snow came.

With so many seasons spent wandering and hunting in the woods, there was little time for book learning. That didn't seem to bother Daniel. He was busy doing what he wanted. It wasn't until his fourteenth birthday that he was taught to read by his older brother's young wife. In a

---

[1] A gunstock is the wooden handle or butt attached to the barrel of a gun. A corn-pounder sweep is a long-armed lever used to lift and lower a heavy wooden pestle that crushes hard corn kernels inside a carved-out log, also known as a hominy block. This was often the way in which settlers made their own coarse cornmeal, which was so important to their diet. A splitting maul is a heavy hammer used to drive wedges to split logs. Trenchers are simple bowls carved from wood.

crude, awkward way, he struggled to write characters with a goose-quill pen dipped in ink. His spelling was his own invention. And when his Uncle John, a learned man, complained of his nephew's wild way with the written word, Daniel's father was said to have replied, "Let the girls do the spelling and Dan'l do the shooting."

What his father said suited Daniel just fine. Next to wandering, hunting was what he liked best. His rambles after wild game led him far and wide, west and north of the Monocacy valley. Of course, he had his own favorite places to hunt. One of them may have been nearby Flying Hill. Here, huge flocks of wild turkeys gathered in such great numbers the very ground seemed to soar when the great, noisy birds were flushed and took wing. From the top of Flying Hill, Daniel could see as far as the range of hazy Blue Ridge Mountains to the west. And what lay beyond that? There was always something inside Daniel that said, Go and find out for yourself.

Sarah Boone knew all about her son's wandering ways. This was not the first time she had waited for Daniel to bring the cows in for milking. But he had never been quite so late before. The forest, already crowded with shadows, smelled of damp night coolness. She had no way of knowing which direction Daniel had gone or what had become of him. She worried that he might be lost or hurt.

There were many unpredictable dangers for a boy traveling alone, even someone like Daniel who had carried his own short-barreled rifle since he was twelve. And before that, Daniel had hunted small game with a sharp, homemade staff cut from a sapling. He had practiced over and over again until he could kill a rabbit at ten yards. Armed now with a rifle, Daniel regularly provided wild game for the family dinner table. He was quickly becoming a better marksman than any of his older brothers.

But still Sarah Boone worried. What if there had been an accident with the gun? Muzzleloaders were heavy, unwieldy, and if not loaded properly, prone to misfire.

It was not uncommon to come upon wildcats and wolves in the high hills. Rattlesnakes and deadly copperheads hid in rocky ledges. And there was always the possibility that Daniel might have met an angry Indian.

Occasionally, hunting bands of Delaware passed through these hills. Until recently, they had been treated fairly by white settlers, both by the first Quakers and years earlier by the Dutch, Finns, and Swedes who'd settled in the land known as Pennsylvania. But now there was cause for uneasiness. The Delaware and Shawnee had been cheated of their best hunting grounds by a crooked land deal known as the Walking Purchase Treaty. They had more than enough reason to be mistrustful of a white face in the forest.

By the next morning, Daniel had not returned. His mother rose early, then searched the forest with a willow switch for the missing cows she could find and herd home. She did the milking and the churning, looking over her shoulder every now and again, expecting that exasperating boy to suddenly appear between the trees. But he never did.

She tied her somber gray bonnet under her chin and hurried barefoot the four miles back to the farm to tell her husband the bad news. Daniel was missing. It would have been difficult for Sarah Boone to conceal her worry. Maybe it was because their summers together had brought Sarah and Daniel closer. Maybe it was because there really was something special that set Daniel apart from the other Boone children. Sarah Boone never hid her feelings. Her sixth child was her favorite.

A search party of neighbors quickly formed. The Quaker way was to help others in need. And everyone was familiar with the Boones. Short, stocky Squire Boone with his bright red hair and stubborn temper was a well-known member of the small group of Quakers belonging to the Exeter Meeting. Tall, Welsh-born Sarah Boone with her dark hair and eyes was considered a devout Quaker all her days.

Daniel had also become something of a familiar figure in the small settlement. He was often seen squatting among visiting groups of Delaware who came to Exeter to trade fur pelts for kettles, cloth, and metal

knives. Daniel always watched and listened attentively, the same way he did whenever Indians visited his home. Sometimes the visiting groups just sat outside, talking together or communicating in signs. They never seemed to mind this curious boy who was slight of build and small for his age with sandy brown hair, pale eyebrows, fair skin, piercing blue eyes, and a wide mouth.

And it was plain to see that there was something Daniel openly admired about the Indians. Perhaps it was their superior knowledge of the ways of the forest. Perhaps it was their skill in hunting. Some people in town may have whispered that it did not seem natural for a white boy to be so interested in these red-skinned heathens, even if, as Pennsylvania's Quaker founder William Penn had said, "We may always live together as neighbors and friends."

The search party combed the hills south toward the Neversink Mountains. There was no sign of Daniel. Finally, on a distant ridge above the pitch pines, someone spotted smoke—the sure sign of a campfire. The search party was said to have found Daniel sitting beside a shelter of sticks and bark, roasting thick strips of bear meat at the end of a stick held over a fire. The savory smell filled the air. Daniel was probably smiling his wide smile.

And why not? He wasn't lost. He knew exactly where he was. Best of all, he had just trailed, shot, and skinned his first bear by himself. If his mother had been frantic with worry, at least now she'd be pleased to have the fine meat and thick bearskin for the family.

What Daniel had done undoubtedly made sense to the search party, made up mostly of backwoodsmen and farmers and not one worried mother. Daniel was becoming quite a hunter, they said. His father should be proud.

Chapter Two

Independent Ideas

It probably would not have surprised George Boone to hear of his grandson Daniel's independent wandering. George Boone had also been a man of fiercely independent ideas. These ideas included "embracing the religion of the Society of Friends," also known as Quakers, and making the long, dangerous journey across the Atlantic to the English colonies in America.

The late 1600s were violent, restless, and uncertain times in England and the rest of Europe. Since the beginning of the century, George Boone's countrymen had continuously fought wars at home and abroad. In little more than sixty years, the English had to obey five different rulers. Each new king or head of state had different ideas, different ways of doing things, different groups of people to favor, ignore, or persecute.

It was a time of tremendous religious questioning. Men and women everywhere were constantly thinking and talking about where and how they could find God. "The name of God was in every man's mouth," one writer recorded. Many of the books that were written, sermons that were preached, and arguments that ended in fistfights centered on this very puzzling question: what was the right way to worship? No one could agree.

In 1702, the Quaker religion appealed strongly to George Boone, a struggling weaver in a small village near Exeter in the county of Devon, England. The thirty-six-year-old father of a growing family was willing to risk everything to practice his new faith.[1]

Becoming a Quaker was a brave thing to do. Quakers were viewed as especially dangerous by English authorities. They questioned not only established religious practice but ideas about government as well. Like other questioners during a time of limited freedom, Quakers were often called traitors.

Between 1650 and 1700, 366 Quakers died while serving time in the dark, disease-ridden cesspools that were English prisons. During this same period, nearly 15,000 Quakers were fined or imprisoned.

Quakers refused to go to war because they believed it was against the teachings of Jesus Christ. They refused to take court oaths or pay required tithes to support the only officially recognized religion, the Church of England.[2] According to the Quaker founder, George Fox, God "was as much at home in house, field, or street as in a building called 'church'." Because of their belief in the equality of all men and women, rich or poor, Quakers kept their hats on, even when they met a nobleman coming down the street. Authorities were even more irritated by the way Quakers used "thee" and "thou" when speaking to everyone—even noblemen and church and government officials.

Quakers purposely wore drab-colored clothing to show they believed

---

[1] The name "Quaker" was originally given as an insult but was eventually proudly adopted by Quakers themselves. The name was first used in 1650 during a trial involving Quaker founder George Fox. Fox had just been brought before the English judge for sentencing.

"Six months in Derby Jail," the judge announced, "and God have mercy on your soul."

"Thou should quake in the name of the Lord," Fox replied.

"Quake?" the judge exploded. "I? Thee, sir, are the quaker!"

With that, the crowd in the courtroom began to chant, "Quaker, quaker, quaker, quaker."

Fox's first followers also called themselves "Children of the Light" and "Friends in Truth." The name Society of Friends was chosen from a Biblical passage: "You are my friends if you do what I command you."

[2] At this time the English government required all citizens to pay part of their wages to the Church of England, whether or not they considered it their religion.

that what was inward was more important than what was outward.*Their meeting houses were plain, too. There were no ministers, candles, choirs, stained glass, or altars. Quakers worshipped together in silence unless a member of the meeting was moved by the spirit to speak.

Basically a cheerful, hopeful religion, the Quaker faith held that every person was inherently good. "God is near to every man with the breath of his life," one early Quaker wrote. In silence during their worship meetings on Sunday, or First Day, as it was called, Quakers were to "try to put aside the problems and disturbances of everyday life. . .and listen for the still, small voice of God, the 'inner light' in their hearts." Outside the meeting house, Quakers made a special effort to practice "good works," to serve others, and to be helpful to anyone and everyone in need—Quakers and non-Quakers alike.

Not until 1682 was there the possibility that Quakers could live and worship without fear of persecution. This was the year a small ship, the *Welcome,* left London carrying one hundred Quakers across the Atlantic to newly created Pennsylvania.[3] Quaker William Penn, son of a wealthy Englishman, had been given this twenty-eight-million-acre tract in the New World by King Charles II to make good on old debts owed to Penn's father, the vice-admiral of the navy.

Penn decided to use the land for what he called a "holy experiment," a place that would allow Quakers and immigrants of other faiths alike to freely practice their own religions. The new government was to be "free to the people under it, where the Laws rule, and the people are party to the Laws." Penn envisioned a justice system that did not permit capital punishment and provided equal treatment for women and people of different nationalities or races. He wanted slavery abolished and equal

[3] Previously, persecution had followed the Quakers even when they had escaped England and tried to settle in the colonies. In Massachusetts, Quakers met with more ferocious hatred than they had known in their homeland. By 1660, the Puritans had hung four Quakers and had beaten, branded, bored through the tongues, or cut the ears off countless others. The religious freedom Puritans sought in the New World obviously did not include anyone with ideas different from their own.

justice for Indians. These were considered very unusual ideas at the time. Many people wondered if such a "holy experiment" could possibly work.

For George Boone, his wife Mary, and many other Quakers, Pennsylvania held great promise. Not only would they be able to practice their faith there without fear, but they'd also be able to purchase cheap and fertile land. And land was what the Boone family had always wanted. Pennsylvania's lure was irresistible.

The problem for the Boones was scraping together the money to make the trip. It took until 1712 for them to save enough from George's poor earnings as a weaver to send their three oldest children overseas. One of those children was sixteen-year-old Squire, Daniel Boone's future father. Squire shipped aboard as a cabin boy. He and his teenage sister and brother sent enthusiastic letters home describing Pennsylvania as a place where good land could be bought for "the cost of a survey and a quitrent a penny an acre; a hundred pounds in cash could buy five thousand acres outright."

The burdensome quitrent system brought over from England became in time increasingly unpopular with land-hungry colonists. It meant that no one could ever own land free and clear. Even after paying for the purchase of a piece of land, colonists by law still had to pay yearly quitrent (or *quit rent*). This was fixed rent payable forever by anyone who bought land from those who had been granted property by the king.

Still, the amount and quality of land that could be purchased in Pennsylvania seemed almost too good to be true. "Because one may hold property as one wishes and pay when one wishes, everybody hurries to take up property," one settler wrote. "In summer one can shoot a deer, dress the skin, and wear pants from it in twenty-four hours." The reports of bountiful crops that could be grown on cleared forest were even more fabulous. "The land," another early settler claimed, "was to be had here for taking up."

Finally, in 1717, George Boone, now fifty-one years old, was ready to make a journey few men his age would have undertaken. He and his wife and six younger children walked seventy miles to Bristol, where they used their hard-earned thirty-five pounds to buy fares to America. They sailed with the next good wind. The difficult trip took nearly eight weeks in a crowded ship with bad-smelling drinking water and spoiled salt pork. The Boones all arrived in Philadelphia in good health. The first boatload of Quakers on the *Welcome* had not been so lucky. Nearly one-third died of smallpox.

In 1720, there were an estimated 466,000 whites and slaves settled in the New World in a narrow strip between Nova Scotia and the Carolinas, as close as possible to the Atlantic seacoast. To the west rose the formidable Appalachian Mountains, and beyond, the mysterious, largely uncharted French territory.

The population was growing by leaps and bounds. Every ship crossing the Atlantic brought more restless, land-hungry settlers like the Boones. They quickly took up claims at the farthest edges of settlement, "where the King's highway ended." Some came seeking fortune and adventure. Others came to find religious freedom. There were also paupers, convicts, and criminals. For these, anything the New World had to offer was better than what they had left behind.

In Pennsylvania, religious tolerance and inexpensive, rich land attracted all kinds of people—German Mennonites, German Baptist Brethren, Swiss Dunkers, Swedish Lutherans, Scotch-Irish Presbyterians, French Huguenots, and German Moravians. In settlements where groups of men gathered in leisure to whittle, chew tobacco, and just talk, it was possible to hear the echoes of many different languages and accents—Scottish, Irish, German, French, and Welsh.

The Boones traveled fourteen miles north along a trace or trail to take up land in a sparsely populated wilderness settlement of Quaker farmers. They stayed and worked together in spite of the hard life and dangers. George Boone moved two more times before he finally settled in Oley Township on a farm of four hundred acres. He was the founder of and became a prominent man in the Oley Meeting, a group of Quakers who met regularly to worship. Eventually, Friend George Boone was chosen as justice of the peace. Later, he even helped name the township of Exeter after the town his family had left behind in England.

Depending on their religion, many men on the dusty main street of Exeter dressed in broad-rimmed, shallow-crowned hats, leather knee breeches or "leggins," wool stockings, and shoes with buckles or moccasins of dressed deerskin. Except for the few who could afford to send overseas for store-bought goods, people made their own clothing. The majority of backwoodsmen wore dull-colored, linsey hunting shirts.[4] This practical, loose-fitting, long shirt was worn wrapped and belted. There was plenty of room inside for a chunk of bread, "jerk" or dried meat, and a piece of tow—or coarse hemp fibers—for wiping a gun barrel. The belt was a handy place to hang a hunting knife in a leather sheath, a bullet bag, or a pair of mittens.

In the Exeter crowd, the majority of the men were clean-shaven. There may have been a powdered wig on the head of a rare visiting lawyer or official, but most men wore their hair plaited or gathered in a club-like knot in back and tied with a ribbon or leather thong—a style that Daniel Boone would one day keep.

Among the women in a frontier settlement like Exeter, the common dress was a linsey gown with a plain bonnet and apron. Most went barefoot during warm weather and wore moccasins or shoepacks after the first frost.[5] Children dressed in the same styles as their parents except that toddlers often wandered about until age three in long shirts.

In 1720, when he was twenty-three, George Boone's son Squire married Quaker Sarah Morgan from a nearby Welsh settlement. They were wed before thirty-nine witnesses in a simple ceremony without a minister. Like his married brothers and sisters, Squire and his new bride settled near his parents. Squire farmed rented land and did a little weaving until

[4] Linsey is a coarse cloth made of linen and wool or cotton and wool. The settlers sometimes wove fast-growing hemp into a cloth that must have been extremely scratchy to wear.

[5] Shoepacks were crude, leather shoes patterned after moccasins.

1730, when he was finally able to buy his own land. The tract adjoined his father's farm. He built a log house and planted his first crop. On November 2, 1734, Squire and Sarah Boone's fourth son was born.[6] They called him Daniel, the name of Sarah's favorite brother.

[6] In Quaker custom, Daniel Boone's birthday was the sixth day of the sixth month. Quakers scorned use of "pagan" names to identify months and days. Identifying Daniel's actual birthday may seem somewhat confusing because the calendars changed during his lifetime. The Gregorian, or New Style, calendar was adopted by most of Europe in 1582 but wasn't put into use in England until 1752. As a result, eleven days had to be adjusted for the Old Style to catch up with the New Style. Daniel Boone's birth date of November 2, 1734, is according to the New Calendar, as are all of the other dates used here.

Chapter Three
Growing Up

Daniel was raised in a Quaker household and was surrounded by Quaker relatives and friends. The influence of this background would remain with him his whole life. However, settlers with peaceful Quaker ideals were beginning to have an uneasy time in the New World.

As the white population increased, surging to the far boundaries of settlement where land was cheap and unclaimed, Indian hunting grounds shrank. Difficulties between settlers and Indians mounted. Whites who had bought, cleared, and plowed claims believed they owned their land. Civilizing the wilderness was viewed by some as a God-given right. Settlers who had made many sacrifices were understandably fierce in defending their farms.

For most Indians, the European concept of land ownership was puzzling. How could a man claim to own something which could not be owned? The Indian way of life was disrupted by treaties that forced them to give up more and more territory, by trade rivalry between the French and English, and by epidemics brought to the New World by the Europeans. Increasingly, the desperate Indians used violence to resist white encroachment.

The harsh reality of bloody attacks and counterattacks by Indians and whites alike forced Quaker settlers to answer a hard question. Should they take up arms to defend themselves even though by doing so they were disobeying their religious beliefs? This was a difficult decision, and there was no real consensus.

While the Boones were peaceful enough, they were ready to fight when they had to. In 1728, a false alarm went out among settlers in Daniel's grandfather's neighborhood. Certain that the Indians were planning a massacre, most people fled. Not George Boone. As justice of the peace, he wrote to the governor, "There remains about twenty men with me to guard my mill, where I have about 1000 bushels of wheat and flour; and we are resolved to defend ourselves to ye last Extremity."

George Boone's stubborn approach was something his grandson, Daniel, took to heart. At an early age, Daniel learned to stand up for what he felt was right and defend himself against what he felt was wrong. A symbol of that was his loose front tooth. As a young boy, Daniel was said to have once had a fierce fistfight with a friend. When the dust cleared, the two fighters made up as soon as Daniel realized their argument was caused by a misunderstanding. But the fight resulted in a tooth that wobbled all of Daniel's life.

How Daniel got his loose tooth was only one of the legacy of stories told about his boyhood in the rolling hills of the Schuylkill valley. Another tale was about fish. Each spring, Squire Boone and his sons fished the river at night with a net for large catches of shad. Enough fish could be caught in a few days for a whole year's supply. The fish were preserved with salt. During one of these fishing seasons, Daniel's mother helped clean the shad the Boones needed and told a poor neighbor family they were welcome to the rest. She returned home, leaving the exhausted fisherman, Daniel, napping on a dry, flat rock, his face covered with his hat.

After a while the neighbor family's daughters came along for the fish. The first thing they noticed was the sleeping Daniel and a bucket of fish heads and guts. The girls lifted his hat and dumped the mess on his head, thinking they'd pulled a funny trick. Daniel did not. He jumped up, wiped the filth from his eyes, and smashed each girl in the face.

With bloody noses, the girls ran home screaming. It wasn't long before their mother appeared at the Boone doorstep to complain.

Sarah Boone, the most devout Quaker in the family, was said to have replied, eyes flashing, "If thee has not brought up thy daughters to better behavior, it is high time they were taught good manners. And if Daniel has given them a lesson, I hope, for my part, that it will in the end do them no harm. And I have only to add that I bid thee good day."

And with that she shut the door.

Daniel's love of wandering revealed itself very early. He turned fretful and unhappy when he had to stay indoors very long. As a little boy at Quaker meetings, Daniel remained only as long as his mother held him by the hand. As soon as she let go, he disappeared. It was said no one ever saw him leave.

The worst kind of confinement for Daniel came when smallpox invaded the little backwoods settlement. Many died from this dreaded disease that spread rapidly from family to family. Without proper medicines or doctors, settlers like the Boones relied on superstition, scant knowledge of some plants and herbs, and quarantine, or confinement. When smallpox suddenly appeared in a neighborhood, parents kept children indoors, as far away as possible from anyone known to have the contagious illness.[1]

At one point, because of the threat of smallpox, Sarah Boone had all her children under strict orders not to leave the house. This was too much for six-year-old Daniel. The little boy quietly talked over a plan with his sister Elizabeth, just two years older. They decided the only way

[1] The scourge of smallpox visited Pennsylvania and the rest of the colonies regularly. Of towns along the Atlantic, Philadelphia, not far from the Boones' farm, was often hardest hit. A passenger or crewman with the virus could arrive undetected and start a contagion. As early as 1730, smallpox inoculation was available and called "a safe and beneficial Practice" by one of its chief Philadelphia supporters, Benjamin Franklin. However, most people were too fearful of this procedure to go through with it.

to get out of the house was to come down with the pox. As soon as they were well, they could go where they pleased again.

That night, after everyone was asleep, Daniel and Elizabeth crept out of bed and ran to the house of a sick neighbor. Quietly, they slipped into bed with the smallpox victim. After lying there for a few seconds, they leapt out again and raced back home. Their secret, they thought, was safe.

It wasn't long before both children showed the first signs of dangerous red spots. Their mother couldn't understand how the two had managed to get sick when they had been so carefully isolated.

Finally, Sarah Boone became suspicious. Looking her little boy full in the face, she said, "Now, Daniel, I want thee to tell thy mother the whole truth."

Daniel told her everything.

She was angry but displayed remarkable tolerance of her favorite son when she replied, "Thee naughty little gorrel, why did thee not tell me before, so that I could have had thee better prepared?"[2]

Luckily, the family and Daniel all survived the smallpox. And just as he had hoped, when he was well again, Daniel was once more allowed to roam as he pleased.

Eventually, wanderlust began to call Daniel's father, too. Squire knew the growing number of immigrants taking up land in Pennsylvania meant that there would eventually be less available for his own children. And season after season of tobacco and corn crops planted in the same fields had caused the soil on Squire's land to lose its richness. Like other settlers, the Boones knew little about fertilizers or crop rotation. Each year's crop produced smaller harvests until the only choice was to move farther into the wilderness, clear the trees, and begin plowing and planting again.

Since he was eight years old, Daniel had heard Boone men tell stories of the wild territory west of the Allegheny Mountains, beyond the Ohio

[2] The word "gorrel" is Old English for youth, lad, or boy.

River, a region unsettled except by dangerous Indians. He also heard tales of the "southwest" as North Carolina was then called. This land was said to be open and untouched, just waiting for the taking by anyone who made the trip to the Yadkin River valley. North Carolina's far western frontier was nearly five hundred miles away on a southern route between the Blue Ridge Mountains and the Appalachians. The game in the rich Yadkin valley was said to be plentiful with "so many bears in autumn that common hunters could kill enough to make two thousand to three thousand weight of bear bacon."

Land was not the only reason why Daniel's father began to think and talk of moving on. There were other troubles as well. With each passing year, Squire Boone was having more and more difficulty with the rules and customs of the local Quaker community.

In 1742, Daniel's eighteen-year-old sister, Sarah, fell in love with a young man named Wilcoxen. He was a "worldling"—someone who was not a Quaker. She married him. This was considered a disgrace in a small place like Exeter, especially when a committee of Quaker ladies discovered that Sarah had been pregnant before her wedding day. Sarah was expelled from the Exeter Meeting, and the Boone family was criticized before the entire group of Quakers for allowing Sarah "to marry out." Squire was recorded as having added "that he was in great streight in not knowing what to do, seeing he was somewhat Sensible that they [Sarah and Wilcoxen] had been too Conversant before."

Five years later, Daniel's oldest brother, Israel, also married a worldling. Israel was disowned at the Exeter Meeting as well. A delegation from the meeting went to Squire Boone's house to speak to him about "countenancing his son's disorderly marriage." The group, which included Squire's own brother James wanted the Boones to apologize publicly again.

Squire refused. He said his children could marry as they pleased. In 1748, the Exeter Meeting records showed: "Whereas Squire Boone hath of late fallen from that good order and Discipline of Friends...

this meeting thinks themselves engaged to give public testimony against him as not being a Member with us until such time as we may be sensible of his coming to a Godly sorrow in himself."

Less than fifty years earlier, Squire's own father, George Boone, had openly disagreed with the Church of England. Now it was Squire Boone's turn to disagree with his religious community. He knew the time was right to move on. But where?

Squire's oldest sister and her husband had already left Pennsylvania and settled in the Virginia River valley. They now had a farm of almost ten thousand acres. The Yadkin River valley also sounded appealing. Reports of its warm, pleasant climate and seemingly endless land that was neither poor nor worn out were impressive.

Squire called his family together. He had decided to sell their property for what he could and leave Pennsylvania. Where they'd settle was not exactly certain. Sarah, who still considered herself a Quaker in good standing, took care to write to meetings in Maryland, Virginia, and North Carolina. Her community of fellow Quakers was important enough for her to carefully collect letters from the Exeter Meeting describing her "merits and orderliness" so that wherever they eventually settled, she could join the local meeting of Friends, if there was one.

In spite of the uncertain destination, two cousins volunteered to make the trek, along with Daniel's best friend, Henry Miller. Daniel was most likely pleased. He and Henry, who was two years older, had worked in Squire Boone's smithing shop together. With Henry's help, Daniel had learned how to repair guns and traps. They had also practiced some other less useful but more amusing skills. Daniel and Henry were well known about Exeter for hanging wagon wheels from barn roofs and making moonlight bareback jumps over sleeping cows.

May 1, 1750—the first day of the journey—would have had all the promise of an exciting adventure to Daniel, nearly sixteen years old. For Sarah Boone, the farewells were perhaps a bit sadder than they were for her son or husband. When would she ever see any of her people again?

Little did she know that the next two years would be spent roaming before the Boones finally put down roots.

The group of travelers may have included as many as ten Boone children: Israel, twenty-four, and his wife; Samuel, twenty-two; Jonathan, twenty; Elizabeth, eighteen; and Mary, fourteen. The four littlest were eleven-year-old George, ten-year-old Edward, six-year-old Squire, and three-year-old Hannah. Although he was six months shy of his sixteenth birthday, Daniel rode in front with the other men. He carried his own Long Rifle, weighing almost ten pounds. It had a barrel forty inches long and a range of nearly two hundred yards. The convoy of crowded covered wagons, barking dogs, and cattle set off eagerly that first day in May; clouds of dust rose up from the road and clung to the dog-toothed violets and brilliant azaleas along the way.

Chapter Four

Ticklicker

During the years spent in the Yadkin River valley, Daniel grew from a boy into a superior rifleman and woodsman. He witnessed a terrible, bloody battle and learned what it took to lead ordinary, yet defiantly independent settlers. He met dream spinners—men who told him tales of Kentucky, that bountiful, mysterious land west of the mountains. And he married the woman who would stay beside him during all the good and bad times that lay ahead.

As they traveled south through the Shenandoah valley from Pennsylvania to North Carolina, the Boones had no way of knowing that two "superpowers" thousands of miles away across the Atlantic were again preparing for full-scale war. After skirmishes by land and sea, the British Crown formally declared war against France in 1756. This time the global conflict centered on the superpowers' North American territories. The consequences would be disastrous for settlers like the Boones in the far reaches of the colonies.

For years, French and English leaders had been headlocked in a struggle of personal ambition. The nearly continuous strife was aptly named: King William's War (1689-1697), Queen Anne's War (1702-1713), King George's War (1744-1748), and the Seven Years' War (1756-1763), known in America as the French and Indian War (1754-1763). The struggle for empire between France and England embroiled other countries as well. At one time or another, Prussia, Russia, Poland, Austria, and Sweden were directly affected in battles fought on land and sea in Europe, Africa, the Philippines, India, the West Indies, and North America. At stake was which country would control more land, more resources, more people.

In North America, France and England could not agree where the other's land claims began and ended. Clinging along the Atlantic coast were the English colonies, teeming with a growing, restless population of one and one-half million, one-fifth of whom were black slaves. New France, as the French called their colony in North America, was inhabited by only seventy thousand Frenchmen. The French territory, named Louisiana, ranged from the Appalachian Mountains in the east all the way to the Rockies in the west, from New Orleans in the south to Quebec and the St. Lawrence River in the north.

To make up for a smaller population and even smaller army, New France needed help from Indian tribes. With lavish gifts, bullets, and gunpowder, the French easily convinced the Shawnee, Cherokee, Iroquois, and other tribes that it was in their best interest to get rid of the white English settlers. Wasn't it true that everywhere the English went, the forests were plowed under for farms and game was scared away?

The key to France's lucrative fur-trading in North America was the Ohio River, which snaked west until it joined the Mississippi River. This was the critical water route the French used to transport furs south to the port of New Orleans and then overseas to European markets. France desperately needed to keep the Ohio River valley for itself. In the view of French trappers and traders, it was only a matter of time before land-hungry English colonial settlers came over the Alleghenies, quickly spread into the game-rich Ohio River valley, strangled the trade route, and established settlements all over Canada.

As the French and English contest escalated, border regions increasingly became the scene of sniping attacks, ambushes, and massacres.

In 1750, two years before the Boones arrived in the Yadkin River valley, the Shawnee struck a group of farms there, killed thirteen settlers, and took ten as prisoners. One neighbor, who had been away during the attack, wrote, "When I came...I found all my family gone, for the Indians had killed five People in the Winter near that place, which frightened my wife and Family away to Roanoke thirty-five miles nearer in among inhabitants."

In spite of Indian attacks, North Carolina's governor claimed that people kept "flocking in daily." Between 1730 and 1750, the population had more than doubled, from approximately thirty-five thousand to seventy-five thousand. Settlers poured into Carolina overland from Virginia, Pennsylvania, and other colonies to the north and by sea from Germany, Scotland, and England.

In the gently rolling western piedmont region of North Carolina where the Boones settled, the land was cheap and easy to buy. Reports about the richness of the soil and the wild game encouraged settlement. "The soil is exceedingly fertile on both sides [of the Yadkin River], abounding in rank grass and prodigiously large trees, and for plenty of fish, fowl and venison, is inferior to no part of the Northern continent," a visiting Virginia official and surveyor wrote. "North Carolina is a very happy Country where people may live with the least labour that they can in any part of the world."

Where the Dutchman's Creek joins the north fork of the Yadkin River, Squire Boone decided to make his claim after arriving sometime in 1752. The Boones lived on the land until April 1753, when Squire finally purchased 640 acres in this area from agents of the earl of Granville. The king of England had given the earl more than half the land that is today the state of North Carolina. Squire's purchase agreement was like that of most of his neighbors. His quitrent of about eight English pounds was to be paid annually forever to the earl, who had rights to three-quarters of any gold or silver that might be found there. Squire was also required to clear and cultivate twenty acres every three years or lose his claim to the land. Quitrents were collected with extreme difficulty (or not at all) by North Carolina representatives of the Crown. The quitrent system was an unhappy reminder of what settlers had struggled so hard to leave behind.

*Eight months later, Squire Boone bought 640 more acres on the other side of the Yadkin. He built a single-story log cabin for his family on a hill overlooking the river. Less than sixty miles distant were mostly friendly Catawba Indians. Beyond the Blue Ridge Mountains, less than fifty miles away, roamed fierce Cherokee.

The nearest settlement was Salisbury, a small, struggling border town some twenty miles distant along the "Great Western Road" from Virginia. Cows roamed freely in this rough-and-tumble marketplace, which also served as the center for local justice. Salisbury residents were very proud of the small, twenty-by-thirty-foot frame courthouse that had just been built, complete with outdoor "pillory, stocks, and gaol."

As they had in Exeter, the Boones quickly became well-known citizens in their new community. While he was certainly not the wealthiest of local farmers, Squire was respected enough to be appointed justice of the Rowan County Court.

Farming had little interest for Daniel, although he helped his father and brothers with the back-breaking work of cutting down trees and grubbing stumps to clear the land. But as soon as it began to rain and outdoor farm work had to stop, Daniel escaped and went hunting. As one of his relatives later remarked, Daniel was "ever unpracticed in the business of farming, but grew up a woodsman and a hunter."

During their journey to the Yadkin, Daniel and Henry Miller had managed to accumulate more than $1,300 in furs and skins by hunting and trapping. They carried these all the way on horseback to Philadelphia to sell. After a week of merrymaking in the big city, they had spent nearly every penny. There was just enough left to bring souvenirs home for their families.

The trip soured sensible Henry on hunting and trapping as a way to make a living. He decided to give them up, and the two friends parted company. Henry stayed in Virginia to found the colony's first ironworks and become very rich and very fat. Daniel moved on to Carolina and never gave up the call of the hunt.

Hunting would one day be his chosen means of livelihood, what one kinsman called "his necessary occupation." Otter and beaver furs brought a good price. A buck deer, prized for the leather that could be produced to make a man's breeches, was nearly as good as money. One buck had the same value as the silver coin known as a dollar. "Buck" and "dollar" in America soon came to be known as the same thing.

Making a living as a hunter was not easy. The job required a high degree of native intelligence, patience, courage, cunning, caution, and unusually sharp senses—the ability to judge distance and distinguish even the smallest differences in sound and smell. A Long Hunter, as a hunter who went into the woods for months on end was called, had to be a better-than-average woodsman. His survival depended on being able to accurately read the weather, the night sky, and animal signs. And, of course, no hunter could manage without luck.

Daniel soon established a fine reputation for himself in North Carolina as a marksman and hunter. Someone said he was such a good shot he could lick a tick off a bear's snout at one hundred yards. Perhaps as a result, Daniel nicknamed his favorite Long Rifle "Ticklicker."

There were, of course, those who made the mistake of trying to take advantage of Daniel. He was friendly and unassuming with strangers. Ever since he was a young child, one relative said, Daniel possessed "amiable traits of character." He was easygoing and likable. But he was no fool. Once in Salisbury, with a horse loaded with furs, Daniel was stopped by two men who had decided he was a simple bumpkin. They suggested a shooting match with a small wager just to make the contest more interesting. Daniel agreed.

The three men went to shoot at targets in a nearby field. Daniel quickly won their ten dollars. Pretending to be very angry about losing his money, one of the men announced that on the next shot he'd beat Daniel. The bet was one hundred dollars against all of Daniel's furs.

Daniel nodded, unaware that the target had already been prepared with a bullet hole next to the bull's-eye. The townsman had only to pull his trigger and claim himself the winner. Daniel watched him take aim and saw him swerve the muzzle away at the last minute. Knowing full well the shot had been a fake, Daniel congratulated his opponent.

Then, with Ticklicker at his shoulder, Daniel squeezed the trigger carefully. The bullet pierced straight through the center of the target. The wager was his.

Daniel's growing reputation as a hunter caused envy, something he would have to deal with the rest of his life. A Catawba sharpshooter named Saucy Jack was tired of hearing white folks brag about a certain Daniel Boone. He decided to do something about it. After too much whiskey, he announced to the world that he planned to track Boone down and kill him. Fortunately, Daniel was off on a hunting trip at the time.

But when Squire heard about the threat to his son, he rushed off in search of Saucy Jack. Forgetting every Quaker principle, he shouted, "If it has come to this, I'll kill first!"

Someone warned Saucy Jack. He fled the valley.

Daniel himself had never met a truly hostile Indian. But times were changing. In the summer of 1754, a Shawnee attack on a settlement two miles from his family's home quickly resulted in a counterattack by white settlers. The French-made guns, beads, and looking glasses found among the possessions of the five dead Shawnee braves served as an ominous warning.

The French were again stirring up the Indians against the English settlements, this time with more vigor than ever.

Chapter Five

Blood
on the Monongahela

The call soon came for Daniel and his neighbors to join the North Carolina militia, a ragtag group of volunteer soldiers who vowed they'd get rid of the French and their Indian allies once and for all. In February 1755, England's Maj. Gen. Edward Braddock arrived in Virginia, ready to lead one of the biggest armies ever assembled in North America.

With flags waving, bugles calling, and bayonets gleaming, the English in their brilliant red coats made loud promises of a quick and easily won victory. "The savages may be formidable to your raw American militia," sixty-year-old General Braddock was said to have told Benjamin Franklin, "but upon the King's regulars and disciplined troops it is impossible they should make any impression."

General Braddock's plan was to capture Fort Duquesne, a key French-held fort overlooking three great rivers, the Monongahela, the Allegheny, and the Ohio. Located near present-day Pittsburgh, Fort Duquesne was considered the most important of a network of forts the French had built to tighten their hold on the Ohio River valley.[1]

[1] The French had already been warned they were trespassing on English land a year earlier, when twenty-two-year-old Virginia militia major George Washington went to the forks of the Ohio with 150 men to garrison a half-built fort. Before they could reach the spot, the French

Thick-set, red-faced General Braddock boasted that bringing Fort Duquesne to its knees would require three or four days at the most. The French and their Indian allies would be routed in no time.

In reality, it took all spring for General Braddock to collect enough supplies and men to begin his attack. The exasperating general demanded 1,500 horses and nearly 125 wagons. Benjamin Franklin came to the rescue with an advertisement sent all over Pennsylvania and surrounding provinces, promising fifteen shillings a day for a team of four horses, a wagon, and a driver. Seven days' pay was offered in advance with the reassurance that "drivers would not be called upon to do the duty of soldiers." Among the drivers who signed themselves up for the job was twenty-one-year-old Daniel Boone.

The monster force of fighting men, wagons, and supplies finally lumbered northwest from Virginia in June. The marching columns totaled nearly thirteen hundred officers and men, two-fifths of whom were American, the rest British. In addition there were two hundred batmen, sutlers, and wagoners and fifty women, mostly soldiers' wives and laundresses who trailed at the end of the line.[2] Thirty wagons stretched for nearly two hundred yards. The sight of the huge army must have been awesome to settlers isolated in the wilderness.

One of Major General Braddock's aides-de-camp was the young Virginian George Washington. Daniel may never have seen the future first president. He and the other wagoners driving with ammunition and food were positioned in the middle of the advancing line of soldiers, officers, artillery, and cattle. Washington rode with General Braddock and his staff in the rear.

Around the evening campfire, Daniel met an Irishman named John

had burned the place to the ground and erected a bigger fort, which they named Fort Duquesne. On July 4, 1754, Washington attacked the French and their Indian allies unsuccessfully near Fort Duquesne. This was the beginning of the French and Indian War.

[2] A batman was a military servant whose job was to lead and care for his cavalry officer's packhorse. A sutler was a person who sold food to soldiers.

Findley (whose name also appears recorded as *Finley*), a teamster who was serving with a company of Pennsylvanians. Findley had been to Kentucky, where he barely escaped the wrath of the angry Cherokee. In spite of the dangers, he was enthusiastic about Kentucky and told fabulous stories of the richness of the land. Here was a place where fortunes could be made! Great herds of buffalo and deer were so tame and plentiful that a man had only to take a stand and the game would come to him.[3]

Findley's campfire tales may have filled Daniel's head as his wagon rolled along on July 9, 1755. It was a warm, lazy, daydreaming kind of summer day. Since dawn, General Braddock's army had been crossing a bend in the Monongahela River. The mood of most of the men was confident, almost jubilant. That afternoon, General Braddock planned to reach Fort Duquesne. The French-held fort would be taken without much struggle, the soldiers told each other. Spies had reported that it was badly undermanned.

Brilliant scarlet uniforms reflected in the shallow water as the British regulars splashed across the Monongahela. "A finer sight could not have been beheld," one soldier wrote. "The shining barrels of the muskets, the excellent order of the men...joy depicted on every face." Daniel must have felt a certain sense of pride in being part of the largest army this side of the Atlantic.

At the same time, he may have been wary. Hadn't there been signs of Indians from the beginning of the march? Careless soldiers who had strayed too far from the main army were easy scalping targets for the unseen enemy. The mutilated bodies of three batmen, a wagoner, and a horse had already been found. Two days earlier, three British soldiers

---

[3] In addition to Findley, two other men on General Braddock's expedition had been to Kentucky. Christopher Gist made the trip in 1750 as a surveyor and explorer. He described it as "a fine, rich level land...full of beautiful natural Meadows...and abounds with Turkeys, Deer, Elks and most sorts of Game, particularly Buffaloes." The year before, Dr. Thomas Walker—also a member of the Braddock expedition—had located the Cumberland Gap, the first in a series of important mountain passes that showed the way west to Kentucky. Whether Daniel met either Gist or Walker is not known.

had been killed in a small skirmish with Indians. When a group of General Braddock's Indian allies returned from chasing the enemy, they were mistakenly greeted by gunfire from British scouts. Just the sight of an Indian made the soldiers panic.

The thick, dark forest on either side of the marching columns was undoubtedly frightening to British soldiers. Even for those familiar with the wilderness, the very trees seemed to have eyes. Indians silently appeared and disappeared. The British regulars heard the American woodsmen-turned-soldiers tell grisly stories of what would happen to any of them unlucky enough to be caught by the enemy. The Indians took no prisoners. There would be no mercy—only scalping and slow, searing torture to the death.

Warfare in the wilderness was completely different from anything practiced in Europe, where obedient, orderly columns marched and fired in unison at an obedient, orderly enemy. The Indians here would not play by the same rules, the Americans warned the British again and again.

But General Braddock and his officers refused to listen. They had been trained to fight in the open with troops in disciplined lines. British regulars had been drilled to obey, not to think. Guerrilla warfare, they had been taught, was for cowards.

Suddenly, a half-mile ahead of Daniel, gunfire rang out. "The enemy!" he could hear men shout. A deadly wave of Indians, French, and Canadians on horseback appeared through the trees, screaming war whoops and firing directly into the advance guard. Later, it was discovered that the ambush party totaled 637 Indians and 254 whites—far fewer than Braddock's force.

A responding volley went out from the British. But the enemy had already disappeared, swallowed up in the black forest. After regrouping, the attackers burst into view again. Now they rode hard down the army's flanks, quickly killing 15 British officers and nearly 150 privates as they went.

General Braddock's troops were paralyzed. As the front of the army began to retreat, the general sent reinforcements forward. The two groups collided in confusion. Officers lost control of their desperate men. American soldiers scrambled for the safety of the trees to continue shooting. In the clouds of gunsmoke, it was difficult to tell who was an enemy sniper, who was an ally.

General Braddock galloped bravely forward as bullets whizzed past from invisible attackers. Five horses were shot out from beneath him before he managed to reach the front of the lines. He shouted at disobedient soldiers who fired at the enemy from behind trees. He waved his sword and struck some of the men to get them to return to orderly ranks. His attempt to rally his troops was useless. The chaos could not be stopped.

From a nearby hill, the Indians and French positioned two of the British army's own six-pound cannons, which had been seized earlier. They blasted away. The air smelled of smoke and death. In less than three hours of fighting, 26 British officers were killed and 714 privates were killed or wounded.

The death toll kept mounting. Finally, word spread that General Braddock had been fatally shot. One of his own officers reportedly had to bribe fleeing soldiers to help carry the fallen leader's body. Retreat seemed the only hope for survival. Men ran or rode as fast as they could back to the Monongahela River ford, "like sheep before the hounds," said Washington, who miraculously escaped death even with four bullet holes through his coat and two horses shot out from beneath him.

Indians chased the men into the water and scalped the stragglers. Terror-stricken, Daniel cut the harness from his wagon and jumped onto the back of one of his horses. He galloped to safety with several other wagon drivers.

A dozen British soldiers unlucky enough to be taken prisoner were marched to Fort Duquesne. With their faces painted black, they were burned at the stake. The French officers present did nothing to stop the Indians' victory celebration.

In a few short hours, General Braddock's proud army had disintegrated into a mass of deadly confusion. The Monongahela flowed red, this time not with the reflected brilliance of fine uniforms, but with blood.

General Braddock's defeat was the worst North American disaster in British military history. The bloody struggle known in America as the French and Indian War would continue for eight more years, with many victories and defeats for each side.

As for Daniel, this was his first taste of the brutality of full-scale war. He had witnessed death, chaos, and the collapse of common-sense leadership when it was needed most. Another eyewitness later wrote, "The yell of the Indians is fresh on my ear, and the terrific sound will haunt me until the hour of my dissolution. I cannot describe the horrors of that scene."

It was a hard, bitter lesson Daniel, too, would never forget.

Chapter Six

Restless Years

As soon as Daniel returned to the safety of North Carolina, he married. Settling down was one way to forget the slaughter he'd seen.

His bride was just seventeen years old. Tall, dark-haired, dark-eyed Rebecca Bryan was the granddaughter of Morgan Bryan, a well-to-do Quaker farmer who had given Daniel's father his job as chief magistrate. Not much is known about Rebecca. She could neither read nor write. All her life she signed her name with an *X*. But she was an amazingly steadfast woman who exhibited a streak of strong will when provoked.

In their fifty-seven years of married life, she would bear ten children and raise nine in all-too-numerous dirt-floored cabins. The family never stayed put long. When Daniel was away hunting or on militia duty for as long as two years at a time, it was up to Rebecca to endure the loneliness, care for the crops, and fend for the children.

Daniel later claimed he had tested Rebecca in courtship for the kind of wandering, uncertain life she'd experience. He tested her for patience. At a cherry picking at the Bryans', the story goes, Rebecca was wearing a lovely white cambric apron—an unusual bit of finery in the backwoods. She and Daniel sat shyly in the grass. It was only the second time they had ever met.

Neither said much. Daniel practiced throwing his hunting knife into the ground. Then he picked up a corner of her pretty apron and began stabbing holes in the precious material. Pick-pick-pick. It must have seemed very odd behavior for a young man in love.

He studied her face. Would she become angry and burst into tears?

Rebecca did not. She held her tongue, perhaps because she understood his little trick. Immediately, Daniel made up his mind. She was the bride for him.

Their wedding on August 14, 1756, was a simple ceremony celebrated with a feast of corn bread, venison, and plenty of home-brewed whiskey. There was no church, nor had a Quaker meeting house been built.[1] As chief magistrate, Daniel's father married the young couple, announcing from the Scriptures, "Daniel took Rebecca and she became his bride, and he loved her." The wedding joined not only Daniel and Rebecca but the fortunes of their two families as well. During the next sixty years, many of the Boones and Bryans would move and settle together wherever Daniel led them, over the Blue Ridge Mountains and beyond.

The newlyweds lived on Daniel's father's property. Their first home was a small cabin with a few acres of cleared land on Sugartree Creek. That spring Daniel and Rebecca's first child, James, was born.

Daniel tried "scratch" farming, as subsistence farming was called, but he never liked it. His land barely provided enough food to feed his ever-growing family. Money for ammunition, coffee, salt, and sugar came from small smithing jobs he performed for neighbors. When he could in the fall or winter, he'd disappear into the forest to hunt and trap.

A successful hunting season might result in upwards of one hundred dressed skins—worth nearly one thousand dollars in today's currency. But Daniel had many expenses. Each of the several rifles, the powder horn, the shot pouch, and the lead and powder he needed all cost money. There were traps, horses, and gunsmithing tools to buy, too. If he was

[1] Without a close-knit, nearby meeting such as he had known in Pennsylvania, Daniel gradually dropped the use of "thee" and "thou" he had been taught as a child.

robbed, as he often was by Indians who considered his activity plain "poaching," he would return home with absolutely nothing.

Daniel was never good at managing his money. It wasn't long before he had to borrow, and soon he was deep in debt. "Boone had the honor of having more [law] suits entered against him for debt than any other man of his day, chiefly small debts of five pounds and under contracted for powder and shot," one of his contemporaries wrote.

Once he paid off the taxes he owed with wolf skins. Occasionally he hired himself out on the local road-building crews to earn money to pay his debts. His father-in-law, Morgan Bryan, probably got him the jobs since he was Rowan County Director of Road Improvement.

As more and more people stricken with land fever arrived in North Carolina, game began to disappear. Daniel had to hunt farther and farther from home. The slow, shivering sigh of falling trees was becoming too familiar. Farms advanced deeper into cleared forests, and problems with Indian neighbors grew.

Since General Braddock's humiliating defeat, some whites had declared open hostility toward all Indians. Terrible atrocities were committed against innocent Indian families. In revenge, the Cherokee nation went on the attack for two years, beginning in 1758. In the spring of that year, it is believed that Daniel joined up as a wagon driver with one of three North Carolina companies on their way to try to take Fort Duquesne again. British brigadier John Forbes, handpicked by Prime Minister William Pitt, led the expedition late in July. His forces were even larger than General Braddock's. The route he selected was over the Alleghenies, across Pennsylvania.

While the army was encamped during the advance, Daniel was said to have killed an Indian. The incident occurred while he was crossing a bridge spanning the Juniata River in south central Pennsylvania. The tall, threatening Indian, the story goes, had a knife and was drunk. Daniel was unarmed. With his shoulder, he butted the brave over the edge of the bridge to the rocks forty feet below. His action may provide a clue to his philosophy of killing only in self-defense. "Daniel never liked to take a life," a friend wrote, "and avoided it when he could."

✻ This time the British conquered the fort, moments after it was blown up by the retreating French. The British rebuilt the place, renaming it Fort Pitt. But the French and Indian War was not over until 1763. Meanwhile, warring tribes made life in the border settlements more unpredictable than ever. When alarms of raids went out, families "forted" together inside barricaded cabins. "The whole family were instantly in motion," one settler recalled, describing an attack in the Yadkin valley in April 1759. He was the eldest in a large family, and it was his job to carry as much food and clothing as he could in the dark. Everyone ran silently without candle or horse to the "fort." "The greatest care was taken not to awaken the youngest child; to the rest it was enough to say *Indian*, and not a whimper was heard afterwards."

Daniel returned safely from the war. In spite of these dangers, he decided to purchase 640 acres from his father on October 12, 1759. On his deed he was listed as "planter," a high-sounding name that did not describe him very well. While Daniel and his family stayed in the Yadkin valley during that dangerous winter, Squire Boone and his wife and youngest children fled to Maryland to stay with relatives.

It was February 1760 when nearby Fort Dobbs, the strongest local log enclosure, was attacked. It narrowly escaped falling into the hands of the Cherokee. With the threat of violence so close to home, Rebecca insisted that they take their two tiny children and move east, too. She was pregnant with their third child when they made the trip that spring to Culpeper, a tobacco-growing town near Fredericksburg in northeastern Virginia. Daniel's younger brother Edward, often called Ned, and his sister Elizabeth and her husband went with them.

While in Virginia, Daniel was said to have met George Washington, a distinguished planter who was active in local politics. Washington was two years older and a full head taller than Daniel.

Restless for the wilderness, Daniel set off on a fall hunt in 1760. He left his brother Ned to take care of his family. In November 1760, his first daughter, Susannah, was born.

It is not known exactly what Daniel did during the next two years. He is said to have crossed the Blue Ridge Mountains with an old slave named Burrell. Burrell stayed with him for a while, but most of the time Daniel was alone, exploring a rocky, open wilderness in eastern Tennessee, "desolate as the day God made it."

On this trip, Daniel may have carved on the bark of a smooth beech tree: "D Boon cilled a Bar on tree in the year 1760." Marking trees with signs was something Daniel did all his life.[2] Some Long Hunters left messages to tell of their danger and frustration: "2300 Deer Skins lost, Ruination by God." Others used trees to signal fresh water: "Come on boys here's good water."

On his return to Culpeper, Virginia, Daniel journeyed through the Yadkin valley, where volunteers were being mustered to fight the Cherokee. He decided to hurry home to Rebecca, sell his furs, and return to the Yadkin to join the Carolina Rangers.

How much action Daniel saw is not certain. The Cherokee War began in 1760 and lasted until 1761 when the weary, starving Cherokee gave up and signed a peace pact, giving up large portions of their eastern lands. Before the conflict officially ended, Daniel may have left the Carolina Rangers and resumed what he liked best—hunting, trapping, and exploring. He roamed all the way to eastern Tennessee with two militia friends, James Norman, a Culpeper neighbor, and Nathaniel Gist, the son of the famous surveyor who had explored Kentucky.

In the spring of 1762, Daniel planted a crop on his land in North Carolina and is said to have remained there through the summer and fall to complete the harvest. Accompanied by his friend James Norman

[2] The authenticity of some beech tree carvings has been challenged. Why would Boone misspell his own name? Some people wonder whether a practical joker roamed the forests carving fake Boone messages. However, most experts agree this message was genuine because it coincides with the date of Boone's visit. The 1760 inscription in eastern Tennessee was recorded as being seen in 1770 and again in 1853 and was later photographed.

he then returned to Culpeper, Virginia, to bring his family back to the Yadkin. According to Norman, Daniel's family had waited nearly twenty months for his return. No one was sure he was still alive.

He was happy and excited in anticipation of seeing his wife and children again. But a surprise awaited Daniel when he entered the cabin, according to the story later told by Norman. There was a new baby girl in his wife's arms. She had been born October 4, 1762.

"Her name is Jemima Boone," Rebecca told her husband.

Daniel's whole world came crashing down. He knew he was not the baby's father.

"She's your brother Ned's."

"Well, if the name's the same, it's all the same," Daniel replied. The subject was said never to have come up between the two again. Daniel accepted the baby as his own.

The family moved back to the Yadkin again to rebuild their cabin and plant a new crop. But Daniel was still restless. In February 1764, he sold his house and 640 acres and moved the family sixty-five miles northeast to the upper Yadkin, near the Brushy Mountains. The next year he moved twice more, trying to find game.

It was with considerable interest that he listened to several of his old friends from the militia tell about a proclamation by the governor of Florida inviting any Protestant settler to receive one hundred free acres. Daniel, his brother-in-law, and his twenty-one-year-old brother, Squire, who was recently married, decided to make the trip along with five other men. They left in August 1765, promising their families they'd be home in time for Christmas.

The journey was a disaster. Game was scarce in the wet and miry swampland. Luckily, friendly Seminole saved them from near starvation. By the time they arrived at St. Augustine and the Florida coast, Daniel's opinion of the land had improved. After they traveled west to the Gulf of Mexico near Pensacola, he bought a house and some land.

The three trudged five hundred miles north again with the good news.

They'd all be moving to Florida, Daniel announced, timing his entrance just as the family sat down to Christmas dinner.

Rebecca was not impressed. In fact, she refused to leave her family and friends. Daniel reconsidered. Well, there weren't much more than alligators to hunt in Florida. He admitted the climate was hot and humid. Maybe his wife was right. The house in Pensacola stayed empty.

Daniel continued farming in the Yadkin. As soon as his oldest son, James, was eight years old, he began accompanying his father on hunting trips. Daniel eagerly taught him the ways of the woods. In bitter winter weather, he buttoned the small boy inside the flaps of his hunting shirt to keep him warm at night. As James grew older, he hunted with his father as long as three months at a time.

While there was game in the forest, Daniel was certain he could make a living and pay back any debt. But he wasn't always able to carry out his plans. On one trip to eastern Tennessee, Indians robbed him. "Ah, Wide Mouth," one of them announced, pulling off Daniel's blanket in the early dawn, "have I got you now?"

Daniel had to think fast. He tried an approach he'd often use with Indians in the years to come. He acted friendly. He discussed hunting and the weather, using Indian sign language. He offered the Indians food. Perhaps his friendly ways saved his life. As soon as the Indians left— with his horse, all his skins, and equipment—Daniel hurried to put as many miles as he could between himself and the braves.

In the little town of Salisbury, North Carolina, merchants to whom Daniel owed money were not so easily charmed by friendly talk. Again and again he found himself in court. Attorney Richard Henderson often defended him. Henderson had known Daniel's father and seemed to admire Daniel.

When they had first met in 1763, Henderson was twenty-eight years old, a year younger than Daniel. The two men were very different. Daniel was a backwoodsman who had never been to school. Henderson was a well-to-do attorney from the Virginia gentry who had married the daughter of an Irish lord. His appearance was striking, he spoke eloquently, and he was a respected member of the bar. Like Daniel, Henderson had dreams about owning land. Unlike Daniel, Henderson had the money to make his dreams come true.

In 1763, Britain had issued a royal proclamation: no colonists were to cross the Allegheny Mountains to clear trees, plant crops, or build homes. In exchange, the Indians were to cease their attacks. Resumed peace would allow the war-debt weary British to engage in a profitable fur trade. The proclamation, Henderson knew, sounded good on paper but was not realistic. There was no way to deter Indian strife or keep the settlers from moving west. Already much confusion existed about the ownership of land west of the mountains because so many land grants had been awarded to veterans of the French and Indian War. George Washington himself wrote to his land agent, "I can never look upon that proclamation in any other light (but I say this between ourselves) than as a temporary expedient to quiet the minds of the Indians. Those seeking good lands in the west must find and claim them without delay."

That is exactly what Henderson had in mind.

As soon as the Indians to the west could be convinced to sell, he and other investors would form a company. They would buy land and establish a colony of their own. But that was in the future. What he needed now was someone brave enough, poor enough, and desperate enough to risk his life to explore for him. That man was Daniel Boone.

Under Henderson's "secret" direction, beginning in 1764, Daniel had made several scouting trips to far eastern Tennessee to meet with Cherokee and to report exactly what their land had to offer. In 1767, he left in the fall with the fellow travelers from his disastrous Florida expedition. This time he was determined to cross the Appalachians and reach Kentucky. The small group pushed over the Blue Ridge Mountains and followed the Holston and Clinch rivers through the Cumberland Mountains. There, they used the Levisa Fork as a guide and hiked a hundred rugged miles to the headwaters of the Big Sandy River. The hunting

49

was excellent. Near a salt lick, Daniel saw and killed his first buffalo. Unfortunately, before they could go any farther, they were "ketched in a snow storm" and had to turn back—not realizing they had actually made it into Kentucky for the first time.

When he returned to North Carolina, Daniel remained restless and disappointed. The expeditions financed by Henderson whetted his appetite for more. Farming in the upper Yadkin valley barely provided enough to eat for his family, which by 1768 numbered six children, with a new baby due the following winter. His debts in town mounted. Game was disappearing. Worse still, trouble brewed close to home.

When the Boones had returned to the Yadkin in 1762 following the end of the Cherokee uprising, they found horse thieves and gangs of cattle rustlers were terrorizing peaceful settlers. Daniel had helped lead a group of angry neighbors in rescuing a kidnapped girl. He had ridden in a posse that captured a band of robbers and recovered stolen property from their hideout.

Now the outlaws were under control, but there was chaos in local government that was difficult to ignore. North Carolina's governor was corrupt. Taxes were unbearably high, and people had lost faith altogether in the court system. At one point, even an honest lawyer like Henderson feared for his life. A group called the Regulators had been formed to protest high taxes and bad government. Unfortunately, they often used violence to get their point across.

In one episode, a law partner of Henderson was beaten with clubs. The sheriff managed to escape by jumping out the courthouse window. For two days 150 rioters roamed through town. They finally left after breaking every pane of glass they could find.

Daniel was uneasy about what was happening around him. He was thirty-four years old, and what had he accomplished? He desperately longed to escape North Carolina. How could he leave? Where could he go? One day in 1768 the answer came riding up to his doorstep in the form of a travel-worn peddler.

Chapter Seven

All the Promise
of Cantuck

It had been nearly fourteen years since Daniel had laid eyes on John Findley, a fellow wagon driver from General Braddock's 1755 expedition. But he still remembered Findley's stories of the glories of Kentucky. Daniel welcomed his forty-six-year-old battle comrade into his home to spend the winter. Findley spent hours at the fireside each night spinning fantastic stories about "Cantuck,"[1] a "new found Paradise" of fertile, rolling plains; endless forests "broke into patches of cane as tall as a man's head;" and, best of all, superb hunting. Findley boasted that Kentucky was crowded with herds of buffalo and deer, flocks of wild geese and ducks, and streams overflowing with fish.

He confided in Daniel that, more than anything, he wanted to see Kentucky again before he died. He knew the way, over the Cumberland Gap, past the Warrior's Path, and northwest to the Rockcastle River. It would be a dangerous journey. The Indians were hostile. What he needed was an experienced woodsmen to help him survive.

Daniel jumped at the "great speck," as he described the profitable

[1] Early spelling of "Kentucky" seemed limited only by the imagination of the writer. *Kaintuck', Kentuck', Cantuckey*, and *Kentucke* are a few of the variations used by Daniel Boone and his contemporaries.

opportunity. The bountiful land and game in Kentucky seemed like an answer to Daniel's prayers. But he needed horses, lead, powder, salt, flour, and blankets. Would Henderson advance the kind of money he'd need to buy supplies? In March 1769, Daniel had to go to court in Salisbury, the county seat. Another creditor was suing him. He took along his brother-in-law, John Stuart, and Findley. It may have been while he was in Salisbury that Daniel convinced Henderson to fund a mission to Kentucky—and to continue to fend off the people to whom Daniel owed money. In exchange, Daniel would identify and explore the best possible claims for Henderson. The expedition would have to remain secret because travel west of the mountains into the Indians' lands was still officially forbidden.

The plan was for Daniel to leave in good spring weather with Findley as guide. The two would be joined by experienced woodsman Stuart. Together, they would hunt, trap, and dress skins with help from three hired camp keepers: Joseph Holden, James Mooney, and William Cooley.[2] Daniel arranged that Squire, his youngest brother, would stay behind to help Rebecca and the family plant and harvest a crop. In late fall or early winter, Squire would meet the hunting party with fresh supplies. No matter that it was nearly two hundred miles into uncharted wilderness; Daniel was confident his brother would find them.

Full of hope and excitement, the six men waved goodbye to their families on a balmy May 1, 1769. And no one was more pleased by the prospects of what lay ahead than Daniel himself. At last he was on his way to the place he had longed to thoroughly explore for nearly fourteen years. As a local preacher once extolled his congregation, "My honeys, heaven is a Kentucky kind of place." Surely Daniel believed that preacher's words.

Pregnant Rebecca may have been less enthusiastic as she stood waving goodbye with a one-year-old baby in her arms and five small children

---

[2] Camp keepers were hired to cook, help keep the camp in order, skin the game, and prepare skins brought back by the hunters.

at her side. Standing next to her, Daniel's youngest sister, Hannah, watched her husband, John Stuart, disappear down the road. In one family, the children would not see their father for nearly two years; in the other, they would never lay eyes on him again.

Kentucky had been explored before, but information gathered about it was not readily available. There were no published maps or guidebooks. Knowledge of the best trails and fords was kept in the minds of men like Findley and only communicated by word of mouth. Even with directions, it was difficult to reach Kentucky. The route had to be found over confusing, rugged mountains, around sheer cliffs, and beyond laurel-tangled ridges that appeared to be dead ends.

For the first part of their journey, Daniel was in familiar territory. The men forded the Holston and Clinch rivers and made their way through the valley of the Powell River. Here was to be found the last lonely white outpost, called Martin's Station. It was an isolated little cabin on the edge of the unfriendly unknown. Now Daniel and the others were dependent on Findley's memory to find the way to the Cumberland Gap.

Warily, they traveled along the Warrior's Path, a kind of secret express route through the Cumberland Gap north and east to the Scioto River. Cherokee and Shawnee often used this path to attack white settlements. At every bend in the trail, the group expected ambush. Luckily, there was no trouble. They kept going, through one long, dark forested valley after another. At last, rising before them in the Cumberland Mountains, was the pass they were looking for—the Cumberland Gap, discovered by Dr. Thomas Walker and named for the Duke of Cumberland. The explorers wound their way to the rocky, tree-covered top.

There, staring far west and north through the haze, Daniel may have glimpsed for the first time Kentucky's distant heartland, the beckoning bluegrass region the Iroquois called "Ken-ta-ke," or "place-of-fields."

The group kept moving, north this time. There was more rugged ground to cover before they made permanent camp and began hunting in earnest. They had still not met up with any Indians. This may have been because so few built villages in Kentucky. The Indians who used this area as a common hunting ground may have been shooting game elsewhere—at least for the time being.

Finally, on June 7, Daniel and his companions set up Station Camp on a fork of the Kentucky River, near present-day Irvine, Kentucky. Their simple shelter was stacked logs on posts, facing the campfire.

Daniel left the other men. He eagerly traveled alone to the summit of Big Hill between the Rockcastle and Kentucky rivers. It was here that he could look down and see the rich, rolling Kentucky terrain that stretched to the western horizon. All the waiting, all the disappointment faded away. He had finally arrived.

In the summer months, Daniel and Findley did more exploring together and then with the other men settled down to the serious business of hunting. They worked in pairs, setting up distant, smaller camps and returning to Station Camp to "jerk" or dry meat and to scrape, cure, and stack deerskins out of reach of bears and wolves. They saw no sign of Indians even though they had located Station Camp dangerously close to the Warrior's Path.

Lulled into carelessness by their good luck, Daniel and Stuart were surprised by a group of Shawnee braves a few days before Christmas. The Indians demanded skins from all the camps. Daniel stalled by taking the Shawnee first to an outlying hunting post. A camp keeper managed to escape back to well-supplied Station Camp with a warning. Daniel hoped the alerted men would quickly pack the bulk of dressed skins—the result of nearly seven months of work—and flee safely. All his money depended on the success of this venture.

His hopes were in vain. Findley and the camp keepers deserted everything—all the deerskins, all the supplies—and disappeared into the forest. Under the leadership of a brave named Captain Will, the Indians took every last pelt, gun, horse, load of ammunition, and bit of food. Daniel and Stuart were held prisoner for two days.

Fortunately, the Shawnee had no intention of killing their prisoners. After a few days, Daniel and Stuart were freed. "Now, Brothers, go home and stay there," warned Captain Will, who supplied each man with moccasins, doeskin to be used for patch-leather, gunpowder, shot, and a small gun. The foolish white men would not starve on their way back to the settlements as long as they could find game. "Don't come here any more, for this is the Indians' hunting ground, and all the animals, skins and furs are ours; and if you are so foolish as to venture here again you may be sure the wasps and yellow-jackets will sting you severely."

The Indians disappeared. Captain Will's words rang in Daniel's ears. That night, he dreamed that bees were stinging him. When he awoke, wondering what his dream might mean, he named the nearby creek Dreaming Creek, a name it still has today.[3]

In spite of the dream's warning, Daniel and his friend decided to track the Indians and boldly steal back their horses, one of which was Stuart's favorite. The two men followed Captain Will's trail and managed to snatch away four horses. They were able to get away undiscovered and rode all night. At dawn, the horses needed to rest and feed. So did the men.

But as soon as Daniel stretched out on the ground to nap, there was Captain Will galloping over the nearby hillock, laughing loudly. "Steal horses, ha?" the brave shouted good-naturedly. He could have killed Daniel on the spot for his audacity. Instead, he tied horse bells on Daniel's neck and ordered him to perform a horse imitation that made him look very silly. Captain Will then announced that Boone and Stuart would have to travel with the Shawnee north to the Ohio River before they'd be allowed to go free.

Angry and humiliated, Daniel and Stuart had no choice but to follow. But at night they escaped into the nearest canebrake. Daniel and

[3] Like many backwoodsmen of his day, Daniel believed that dreams could foretell the future. He once said that if he dreamed of his father and his father was angry, it meant something terrible would happen. But if his father seemed pleasant, he had nothing to fear.

Stuart listened as the Indians discovered their loss; then they kept still and waited. There was no way the Indians could find their captives in the head-high cane. At last, the Shawnee gave up.

Meanwhile, Holden, Mooney, Findley, and Cooley were traveling as fast as they could back to the settlements. One account says that on their way they met Squire Boone and a young friend named Alexander Neely, who had come with supplies. The group camped, arguing whether to escape with their scalps or return to look for Daniel and Stuart.

Just as they sat down to eat, they heard a noise.

Two bearded intruders in tattered clothes took cover behind trees and shouted, "Hello, strangers. Who are you?"

"White men and friends!" came the reply.

Luck seemed to be with Daniel again! He and Stuart were overjoyed to see Squire and hear word about their families. Daniel forgave the deserters and eagerly suggested new plans. This time they would set up camp safely away from the Warrior's Path.

Findley, who was ailing, shook his head. He and the camp keepers had had enough. They were going home. Daniel watched the four men disappear into the forest, Findley in the lead. It was the last time he saw the old Irish dream spinner.

The four who remained established a new camp on the north side of the Kentucky River. In addition to news, Alexander Neely had brought along a book. Around the campfire, he read aloud from *Gulliver's Travels,* much to Daniel's delight. Daniel enjoyed a good travel story, especially one nearly as fantastic as the adventure they were experiencing.

Just as they were hearing about Gulliver's visit to the city of Lorbrulgrud, Indians appeared between the trees. Luckily, the men were able to frighten them away with harmless gunfire. Neely laughed when the incident was over, boasting they had made quick work of the citizens of Lorbrulgrud. Ceremoniously, they named the nearby creek "Lulbegrud" Creek, a name it still bears today.

To hunt and trap, the four men divided into two pairs: Squire and

Neely, Daniel and Stuart./Daniel and Stuart worked especially well together. Daniel once told one of his children that "he never had a brother he thought more of than he did of John Stuart." In January, the pair agreed to meet after a week of hunting and trapping. On the appointed day, Stuart did not appear. Worriedly, Daniel ranged the woods, searching and calling for his friend, who he knew had crossed south of the swollen Kentucky River. At last, Daniel was forced to give up. He returned to tell the others the sad news.[4]

The news was too much for Neely, who left for home. Kentucky seemed every bit as dangerous as he had been warned.

That left Daniel and his brother. They continued to hunt, but they were even more careful now. They cooked at night so that the smoke from their fire would not be detected and went so far as to create a secret entrance to their camp.

The following spring, their ammunition supply began running low. Someone had to return east to purchase lead and powder. The brothers had accumulated a good store of dressed skins and were hopeful the Kentucky venture might turn a profit after all. Squire volunteered to make the trip back to Salisbury with the loaded packhorse. He promised to sell the skins, pay off as much of Daniel's debts as he could, give word to Daniel's family that he was still alive, and return with supplies.

Daniel had promised Henderson he would explore the land thoroughly—dangers or no. Without a dog, horse, bread, salt, or sugar, Daniel remained alone in the wilderness. Later, when asked if he wasn't afraid to venture into an unknown part of the forest, he was said to have replied, "Sure am. I wouldn't give a hoot . . . for a man who isn't sometimes afraid. Fear's the spice that makes it interesting to go ahead."

And go ahead he did. For the next three months, Daniel ranged the mountains and hills as far as the Ohio River, nearly a hundred miles

---

[4] What was believed to be Stuart's skeleton was discovered years later, perched inside a hollow sycamore tree. The skeleton's left arm was broken, but there were no other injuries. A powder horn found nearby was inscribed with Stuart's initials.

north. He slept in canebrakes at night to conceal himself from Indians. Often he camped in Kentucky's many caves. In the soft stone wall of one he carved: "D.B.—1770."

Squire kept his promise. After safely transporting and selling the skins, he rejoined Daniel on July 27. He reported the birth of Daniel's third son, Daniel Morgan, who had been born just before Christmas. With fresh supplies and ammunition, the two brothers hunted and trapped along the Kentucky River. At one point, a pack of wolves tracked them. A big gray male grabbed Daniel's favorite felt hat and ran. Daniel shot the wolf because he did not want to lose his hat. In the wolf's den, the men found new kits. They tried to raise them as pets, without success. "A wolf's always a wolf," Daniel later told one of his grandsons.

As autumn approached, Squire again returned to Salisbury to sell more skins. Daniel waited patiently for his brother's return. When it seemed to be taking too long, he started after him. Years later, he told how on this trip he came upon an aged, sick Indian who could no longer travel and had been left to die by his tribe. Daniel felt sorry for him. He traveled a half-mile to where he had killed a deer and brought fresh meat for the old man.

Squire finally reappeared. The second load of skins had made it through. The expedition was turning into more of a success than Daniel had ever imagined. He'd seen and explored Kentucky to his heart's content. He had much to report to Henderson. With one more load, they'd be ready to go home to their families again.

Daniel must have been feeling pleased with life. The sound of his loud singing scared another famous Long Hunter half to death. Caspar Mansker, who had been hunting farther south for nearly a year and a half, told how he and a small group of companions were creeping through the forest after being robbed by Cherokee of more than five hundred skins. Mansker assumed the remarkable noise he heard was an Indian decoy. Not wishing to take any chances, he slunk from tree to tree to investigate. There on a deerskin was Daniel Boone, bareheaded and stretched flat on his back, all alone, singing happily at the top of his lungs.

In March 1771, Daniel and his brother started back, their horses loaded with skins. They reached the Cumberland Gap in May and were not far from home—when who should stumble into view but Neely! He had been lost since he'd separated from another hunting party from the Powell River valley. He had shot off all his ammunition trying to signal for help and was now nearly starved. He had only eaten a stray dog he had somehow managed to trap and kill.

Daniel and Squire shared provisions with him. As they ate, they were joined by six or eight Indians. The braves seemed amiable enough, so Daniel generously invited them to share their roasting meat. Soon the Indians demanded all the hunters' guns, supplies, and furs. Outnumbered, the three men could only do as they were asked.

Everything they had worked for over more than half a year was gone. Daniel, Squire, and Neely tried to chase the robbers, but the Indians quickly alerted reinforcements. Daniel turned back, barely avoiding a deadly ambush. They had come too far to lose their scalps just a few short miles from home.

The two scraggly, bearded Boone brothers trudged home. Daniel returned without a horse or a gun and stripped of six months' hard work. It was not a particularly triumphant entry. Even with the two loads of furs that Squire had sold, Daniel still owed everybody in town money. He had left his farm and family and risked his life for two years. What did he have to show for it?

What Daniel had gained was first-hand knowledge of a land that was everything he had dreamed, yet was still just out of reach. Even as he hurried to embrace his family, he knew that in spite of all the hardships, he would not be satisfied until he returned.

Chapter Eight

Journey into Darkness

There were men who could not rest until they lived in Kentucky. One of them was Daniel Boone.

Upon his return, Daniel tried to convince Richard Henderson that the time was right for settling Kentucky. He was not successful. Henderson was enjoying a position on the highest court in North Carolina and, in 1771, his term had two more years to run. His lucrative law practice was expanding and involved his making lengthy trips across the colony. He was perhaps more aware than Daniel of the growing tension between colonists and the Mother Country. Some people were already talking about war. The British might soon be too preoccupied to notice what went on in distant Kentucky. Have patience, Henderson told Daniel.

But patience was something Daniel lacked, especially when it came to following written rules—a fact which may have explained why he was so often in court. For almost seven years, he had been secretly employed by Henderson to explore and survey Kentucky and parts of present day Tennessee. Daniel had met with friendly Cherokee to see if they might be willing to sell Henderson their hunting grounds. Still, Henderson refused to begin negotiations in earnest.

Daniel's impatience grew. In Kentucky, he was convinced, a man could be free from quitrents and taxes, lawsuits and creditors. In Kentucky, he could make his living hunting and trapping. In Kentucky, he might find the land he hungered for.

Daniel knew, however, that without financial backing, he could not strike out for the fabled bluegrass region. He was broke. He realized, too, that taking his family alone into Kentucky meant risking their lives. No one could be sure the Indians would not attack.

Little is known about what Daniel did during the next two years. Records show that in 1772 he packed up his belongings and with his family moved to Sapling Grove in what is now western Tennessee. Then he moved back, this time to the upper Yadkin valley.

In 1773, once again as Henderson's agent, Daniel went exploring in Kentucky with a few hunting friends. He talked with Cherokee, often discussing the hunting and the weather as they shared a meal together. The conversation, Daniel made sure, eventually included a discussion of land. Were the chiefs willing to sell? Daniel did not forget those who seemed interested in the idea.

As he continued on his travels, he visited many of the same places and camped in many of the same caves he had found in 1770. By now routes to Kentucky—overland through the Cumberland Gap or by flatboat down the Ohio River—were generally known. Daniel met surveyors, adventurers, and Long Hunters; all seemed determined to settle in Kentucky in spite of the law. Would the good land soon be gone?

On their way back home to the Yadkin through the Clinch River valley, Daniel and his companions stopped in Castle's Woods, a raw little collection of log cabins in far western Virginia. There they met thirty-eight-year-old Capt. William Russell who had settled Castle's Woods a few years earlier. Captain Russell had built a large house and owned several slaves. For his heroic service in the French and Indian War, he was one of many soldiers to be granted a sizable tract of land in Kentucky.[1]

[1] When the Royal Proclamation of 1763 redrew the boundary separating white man's country from Indian territory, the veterans' rights to their land became unclear.

Russell's Kentucky claim was of great interest to Daniel. Had Captain Russell ever been to Kentucky?

No, he replied, he had not.

This was all the prompting Daniel needed. He told Russell everything he knew about that wonderful place. His stories of the land's richness convinced not only Captain Russell but Castle's Woods residents David Gass and Michael Stoner as well. They all agreed to start a new settlement in Kentucky, in spite of Indian dangers and royal proclamations.

Captain Russell hired Daniel as guide. What promise Russell may have made regarding Daniel's share of the land is not known. However, Daniel must have been pleased with the arrangement because he rushed back to tell Rebecca the good news. They'd sell every bit of land they had on the upper Yadkin and whatever belongings they couldn't carry. At last, they were taking the children and moving to Kentucky!

Daniel's enthusiasm convinced his brother, Squire, several of Rebecca's relatives, and a few neighboring families to join them. On September 25, 1773, as the trees began to blaze with brilliant color along the Blue Ridge Mountains, the Boones, their relatives, five other families, and a few slaves were on their way,[2] accompanied nearly half a day by other North Carolina neighbors who wished to see them off.

Daniel's seventy-three-year-old mother was among those who made the trip to say goodbye. When a halt was finally called for the separation, Sarah Boone was said to have thrown her arms around her favorite son's neck and cried bitterly. It was a sad farewell. Even Daniel was seen

---

[2] The majority of Quakers, especially those living in northern colonies, were against slavery. However, slavery existed extensively in Virginia on large plantations. Many of the settlers who could afford to purchase slaves brought them with them as they moved into western Virginia and over the mountains into Kentucky. For the most part, the Boone family was too poor to have slaves. In 1787-1788, when Daniel had filed claim to nearly one hundred thousand acres of Kentucky land, he was known to have the most slaves he ever owned: three. In his old age, he traveled and hunted extensively with a young male slave. His wife, Rebecca, was said to have been buried beside a favorite slave. Slavery was not officially abolished in Kentucky until 1865 with the passage of the Thirteenth Amendment.

drying his eyes. It is not known if they ever saw each other again. In four years, Sarah Morgan Boone would be buried beside her husband in Davie County, North Carolina.

When Daniel's followers joined Captain Russell's family and friends in Castle's Woods, there were more than thirty well-armed men plus women and children.

Travelers at this time took many different routes to reach the Cumberland Gap, which opened the way to Kentucky. All of these routes involved first crossing a series of mountains and valleys that rose and fell like ridges on a wrinkled blanket, all angled from northeast to southwest. Marching in single file, Daniel and the others moved along a southwesterly route to the Cumberland Gap, following buffalo traces, streambeds, and Indian trails across the Clinch and Powell mountains. They reached the Powell River valley and kept moving. The plan was to then follow Wallen's Ridge all the way to the Cumberland Gap.

Because there were no roads, they brought no wagons. Children too young to walk rode, wedged between rolled bundles on the backs of packhorses. Older children carrying long switches helped coax the stubborn cows through the trees, beat the ground for poisonous snakes, and watched carefully for ground nests of bees that could stampede the livestock. It was slow going, especially when frightened cattle and horses suddenly bolted into the woods, sending supplies flying. Hours might be spent collecting all the scattered goods.

With pans clanging and the butter churn rattling against the plowshare, each packhorse carried on its back all that one family would have to eat, cook, sleep, wear, and farm with during the coming year. Rebecca had packed her entire family's clothes in one deerskin satchel slung over her saddle horn.

Like beads on a string, the travelers gradually spread out along the trail and divided into three loosely formed groups. At the lead was Daniel with the women, children, baggage, and most of the cattle. In the middle were Daniel's eldest son, sixteen-year-old James, and Captain Russell's

eldest, seventeen-year-old Henry. The boys were accompanied by two young brothers, James and Richard Mendenhall; two white laborers, Isaac Crabtree and a man known simply as Drake; and two Russell family slaves, Charles and Adam. This middle part of the caravan carried flour, farming tools, and some books and drove a small herd of cows. Bringing up the rear were William Russell and David Gass.

The travelers were still not far from St. Martin's Station. A group who had just passed them going east had told of friendly Indians ahead who had even shared their meat. On October 9, the first two groups pitched camp three miles from each other on Wallen's Ridge in present day Lee County, Virginia, just a day's walk from the Cumberland Gap.

As darkness fell, James and Henry's party huddled near the campfire. The forest's eerie sounds were punctuated with the hair-raising howling of giant timber wolves. Were they real wolves or Indians calling to one another? Crabtree taunted the frightened Mendenhall boys—this was nothing compared to the sounds they'd hear in Kentucky, where, he said, wild buffalo bellowed from the treetops.

Uneasily, the boys spread their blankets on the ground. The night was spent in fitful sleep.

Just before dawn, Indian gunfire burst through the trees. The two young Mendenhall brothers and Drake were killed instantly. Charles was led by the Shawnee into the woods, where he was also killed. Crabtree was wounded and escaped through the forest. Adam scrambled for safety into a pile of driftwood on the banks of Wallen Creek. He watched in terror at what happened next.

James and Henry, shot through the hips, were unable to move. The band of Shawnee included an Indian whom James recognized. He was Big Jim, a man who had visited the Boone home. James called Big Jim by name, begging him to spare his life. Big Jim refused. Slow torture was what the Shawnee had in mind.

Adam listened helplessly to the boys' screams. Their bodies and faces were slashed to ribbons. Their fingernails were torn out. The palms of their hands were sliced as they tried desperately to push away the Indians' knives. Again and again, they pleaded to be tomahawked to end their awful suffering. But the torture continued until both were dead. The Shawnee took scalps, left behind a war club as a sign of defiance, and rode off with the horses and supplies.

It was Captain Russell and David Gass who stumbled onto the scene and found the bodies. In horror, a runner rushed to tell Daniel. It's difficult to imagine the shock and sorrow felt by everyone, but especially by Russell and Daniel, who were responsible for leading the caravan. Daniel made the women and children take cover in a ravine near a washed-out beech tree. He posted sentinels in case of another attack.

Rebecca took her best linen sheet—she had hoped to use it in her new home in Kentucky—and sent it back to wrap the boys for burial. James and Henry shared a single grave. Stones and dirt were tramped down to discourage hungry wolves.

The rest of the day and all night, the group waited miserably in the ravine for another attack. In the morning, they had no stomach to go on. Kentucky was too dangerous. Only Daniel wanted to keep moving. He had sold everything, and he and his family no longer had a home to return to. No one wanted to go with him.

David Gass generously offered the Boone family the use of one of his cabins at Castle's Woods. Daniel agreed. Filled with fear and despair, the ragged group filed home, some to North Carolina, others back to Virginia. Daniel was defeated—again.

The news of the massacre quickly spread to the already nervous border settlements. A report sent to the governor of Virginia was printed in the *Virginia Gazette* in Williamsburg, where Captain Russell was well known. "Indians killed young Mr. Russell, four white men, and one negro," the report said, never mentioning Daniel or his son. Daniel Boone was not yet the household word he would one day become.

Grisly evidence of the murders began to surface. A stolen horse was identified in Pennsylvania. One of Captain Russell's books turned up in the hands of an Indian trader. An unfortunate result of the publicity was heightened hatred of Indians. Two Shawnee chiefs, who had purportedly been on the scene, were put to death by officers of the governor of Virginia. Crabtree, who had been wounded and barely escaped the attack, began having delusions about revenge. At a horse race the following year, he killed an innocent Indian spectator in cold blood. He was never tried in a court of law.

For the next two unhappy years, Daniel and his family remained at Castle's Woods in a house they did not own, in a place they did not want to be. War simmered all along the frontier. By May 1774, the Shawnee were fighting along the Ohio River to the north. Meanwhile, the Cherokee were attacking border settlements in present-day Tennessee to the south. It was not a good time to venture far into the wilderness.

In spite of the risk, Daniel returned in the spring of 1774 to James's grave. It was undoubtedly the very lowest point in Daniel's forty years, a time he would one day look back on and call "the worst melancholy of my life." He discovered that animals had tried to dig away the dirt. He reburied the bodies and placed heavy logs over the common grave.

For hours, Daniel sat in the gloomy forest, head bent, just staring. All his dreams, all his ambitions seemed buried there with the son he had loved so much. It was James he had taken into the forest on hunting trips since he was a little boy.

"James was a good son and I looked forward to a long and useful life for him, but it is not to be," Daniel later wrote in a letter. "Sometimes I feel like a leaf carried on a stream. It may whirl about and turn and twist, but it is always carried forward."

A sudden gust of wind blew around Daniel. In a few minutes, it was raining hard. Thunder boomed, and lightning flashed overhead. He took shelter in the trees. When the storm finally lifted, he built a fire and camped nearby, "hoppling" his horse with a bell so that he could hear where it was in the thick forest as it grazed.

Daniel did not know that he had been followed in the darkness. Now his sharp ears suddenly picked up the sound of movement—Indians approaching. Quietly, stealthily, he crept to the horse. He led it quickly away, taking care to ring the bell every now and again to make it seem as if the horse were still grazing. When he finally felt safe, he silenced the bell, leapt on the horse's back, and rode as fast as he dared back to the settlement.

Chapter Nine

Lord Dunmore's War

When Daniel returned to Castle's Woods, a new job awaited him. He was to travel as quickly as he could back to Kentucky to warn and guide home a party of surveyors who were in serious danger. They were neither properly armed nor aware that the Shawnee and Mingo were on the warpath. The corrupt governor of Virginia, Lord Dunmore, had personally sent the surveyors to the falls of the Ohio River and the bluegrass region near present-day Lexington, Kentucky, to divide the land for his own profit.

The rescue assignment had been handed to Col. William Preston, Dunmore's western Virginia militia commander, who in turn passed the job to Captain Russell. Russell sent word June 26, 1774, that "two of the best Hands I could think of, Danl Boone, and Michl. Stoner... have [been] Engaged to search the Country, as low as the falls, and to return by way of Gaspers Lick on Cumberland, and thro' Cumberland Gap."

Indian trouble had flared along the frontier border all spring and early summer as more and more land seekers spilled over the mountains, completely ignoring royal proclamation boundaries. There seemed to be no way to stem this rising tide. For many people along the Atlantic seaboard, life was becoming difficult as tensions mounted between the Mother Country and its colonies. It had been nearly a year since a group of townsmen dressed as Mohawk tossed 342 chests of fine English tea into Boston Harbor. More colonists were talking revolution. Neighbor mistrusted neighbor. Moving west was a way to escape overcrowding, hostility, and bad politics.

Lord Dunmore caused more troubles. He wanted to own vast expanses of land west of the mountains. He stirred up the Indians' hatred of the white settlers; then, when the angry tribes attacked, Dunmore sent troops to help the settlers fight back. The hoped-for result? Annihilation of the Indians and their land claims.

The brunt of the brutal Lord Dunmore's War, as it was mockingly called, was borne not by the royal governor, of course, but by Indians and by settlers—people like Daniel, his family, and his neighbors.

On June 27, 1774, Daniel and Michael Stoner started into the wilderness, probably on foot. No one knew exactly where the surveyors were. But if anyone could find them, Captain Russell had promised, it was Daniel and his short, stocky companion, called by some "the best shot in Kentucky." Stoner, a Castle's Woods settler, had been along on the disastrous expedition to Kentucky with Daniel's family. Born in Pennsylvania Dutch country, Stoner had a thick German accent and a pair of arms so muscular it was said that he could carve his name on a tree while carrying a three-hundred-pound pack on his back. Daniel liked Stoner. He was a good hunting companion. Together, they ranged the country at night to avoid being seen by Indians. They traveled over the Cumberland Gap to the falls of the Ohio River, near present day Louisville. In late July, they came to Harrodsburg, the first little settlement built in Kentucky. Mysteriously, the place was abandoned.[1]

Daniel and Stoner did not know that on July 8, Indians had attacked and killed two men. The rest of Harrodsburg's inhabitants and part of the original group of Dunmore surveyors had fled east.

[1] James Harrod and thirty-two men left Pennsylvania in March 1774 and came down the Ohio River in canoes and then traveled overland to found Kentucky's first settlement. In June 1774, they began marking off sites for Harrodstown, later named Harrodsburg.

Unaware of the attack, the rest of the surveyors had split into three groups to cover more territory. It was not until August 26 that Daniel and Stoner discovered several of the men and accompanied them back to Castle's Woods.[2] In sixty-one days, the two woodsmen had covered nearly eight hundred miles.

When Daniel and Stoner returned, they found most of the Clinch River men had gone to fight with the militia, as commanded by Lord Dunmore. Before Daniel and Stoner could join them, they were ordered by Captain Russell to stay behind to protect the women and children and guard the houses and farms from attack.

A chain of three small "forts"—Blackmore's Fort, Moore's Fort, and Russell's Fort—had been hastily constructed along the Clinch. These barricaded courtyards and buildings were where people from surrounding farms went for protection. Daniel did such a good job keeping order and protecting the people that he was voted to command the garrisons at all three forts. He was even given the title of captain. Daniel seemed to inspire confidence among the frightened groups huddled in the frontier outposts. Because his own family had left their home for protection at Moore's Fort, the settlers reasoned, Captain Boone would never desert them.

Not all the men on fort duty viewed their job as Daniel did. During the warm, early fall days of 1774, many lounged about in the grass outside, napping or playing ball. Once, while Daniel was away on a scouting mission, only one man dutifully remained inside the fort walls. Rebecca and six other women decided to teach the careless guards a lesson.

They carefully loaded guns with a small amount of powder so that

[2] Two parties of surveyors at work not far from Harrodsburg eventually returned there on July 24, only to find the place eerily abandoned. Nailed to a tree was the message: "Alarmed by finding some people killed we are gone down this way." The forewarned surveyors returned home safely. Nine other surveyors led by Hancock Taylor weren't so lucky. On July 27, they were traveling by boat down the Kentucky River when they were attacked by Indians on shore. Two men, including Taylor, were killed. Lost and without a leader, the surveyors fled into the forest. This was the group that Daniel and Stoner discovered.

when fired, they would sound like Indian guns. Then the women scurried outside the fort where the men could not see them and rapidly shot off the rifles. Lickety-split, they ran back inside and slammed the gate shut.

Panic! The alarmed men were certain it was an Indian attack. They could not get into the fort. Some fled straight to the woods. Others were said to have tumbled into a nearby pond for protection. Only one managed to climb the fort wall. And when the men realized it was all a joke, they were so enraged they threatened to whip the women.

It's doubtful they frightened Rebecca, however. She watched with satisfaction as the angry men's quarrels led to fistfights among themselves.

Lord Dunmore's War came to an end after a fierce battle on October 10, 1774, at Point Pleasant in what is today West Virginia. The battle of Shawnee against settlers raged all day, with terrible losses on both sides. Finally, Chief Cornstalk surrendered and signed a peace treaty. The men in the militia returned to their farms and families.

But there were no peaceful times ahead. Far-reaching changes were taking place in the colonies. Royal officials were quietly buying passages back to England. They had had enough of rowdy, ungovernable colonists. The very troops that Lord Dunmore had used to fight the Indians would soon be turned against him, in the American Revolution.

Chapter Ten

Kentucky:
New Sky, Strange Earth

With the end of Lord Dunmore's War, Richard Henderson finally felt bold enough to disobey the royal governors and go ahead with his Kentucky land scheme. And why not? The British were so busy dealing with rebellious colonials that no one had time to squash the "illicit and fraudulent" activities of Henderson's new land company, the Transylvania Company. His tenure as judge completed, Henderson and his two business partners, Nathaniel Hart and John Luttrell, decided the time was right to move quickly. In exchange for two thousand acres of good bluegrass land, would Daniel help negotiate with the Cherokee and lead the road-building crew to Kentucky?

Daniel did not hesitate. He immediately returned to Kentucky for friendly meetings with all the chiefs he had been trying to interest in selling claims since 1773.

Although most of Kentucky still officially belonged to the earl of Granville, Henderson and the other Transylvania Company partners planned on directly purchasing twenty million acres from the Cherokee to create a new, fourteenth colony, called Transylvania, to govern as they wished. They'd keep the best land for themselves, make a small fortune selling what was left to settlers, and collect quitrents for their heirs "forevermore."

What Henderson proposed was so bold, so incredible, so illegal that when one North Carolina official heard of it, he wrote: "Pray, is Dick Henderson out of his head?" Governors of both North Carolina and Virginia declared the scheme "daring, unjust, and unwarranted." What they said, however, no longer mattered. Official attention was turned toward the trouble between Britain and the colonies. By April 1775, the American Revolution was in full swing.

Now Henderson began negotiations in earnest. Six wagons loaded with guns, shirts, blankets, and trinkets worth nearly eight thousand pounds were hauled from North Carolina to Sycamore Shoals in Tennessee for the Cherokee to see. Another two thousand pounds sterling was promised when an agreement was reached. By Christmas, Henderson was already advertising "for settlers for Kentucky lands about to be purchased."

In March 1775, Henderson, his partners, various interpreters, a white attorney for the Indians, and more than one thousand Cherokee gathered at Sycamore Shoals for treaty negotiations. There was plenty of meat and corn to keep everyone happy. Rum was to flow freely only after the official treaty was signed. Henderson opened the talks by attempting to make sure the Cherokee owned the land they were selling. Ancient Chief Atacullaculla (Leaning Wood), leader for more than fifty years, claimed it was theirs.

His son, Dragging Canoe, carefully examined the map Daniel had drawn to show the new land boundaries. At first Dragging Canoe refused to sign Henderson's treaty. He understood that it meant the Cherokee were giving up valuable land and would eventually forfeit their way of life. "The whites have passed the mountains and settled upon Cherokee lands, and now wish a treaty," he protested. "When the whites are unable to point out any further retreat for the miserable Cherokee, they will proclaim the extinction of the whole race...Such treaties may be all right for men too old to hunt or fight. As for me, I have my young warriors about me. We will have our lands."

It was said to have been Daniel who spent hours trying to persuade and cajole Dragging Canoe. Daniel agreed that the white man's numbers were growing. Wouldn't it be in the best interest of the Cherokee to sell part of their land to a friend like Henderson rather than risk everything in battle? Dragging Canoe finally agreed, but he had the last word. "Brother," he reportedly told Daniel, "we have given you a fine land, but I believe you will have much trouble in settling it...There is a dark cloud over that country." His warning referred to the angry Shawnee. No one, not even Daniel, realized how true his prophecy would be.

The Treaty at Sycamore Shoals was signed on March 17, 1775. Henderson and his Transylvania Company purchased ninety thousand square miles for approximately fifty thousand dollars in colonial currency. In addition to land drained by the Cumberland and the Kentucky rivers east to the mountain barrier, they now owned rights to build what would be called the Wilderness Road, a route through Indian territory to the heart of the Transylvania Company's new Kentucky empire.

Daniel was not present to watch the final treaty signing. A week earlier, as leader of the road-cutting crew, he had left Sycamore Shoals to meet thirty other men to begin clearing the way for the Wilderness Road.[1] It was a convenient time for Daniel to disappear. Once again, he owed people money. Soon after the first road builder's ax rang through the forest, a warrant was issued against Daniel's property. Of course, nobody could find him. Across the back of the April 19, 1775, arrest warrant an official wrote, "No goods" and "Gone to Kentucky."

That same day, 130 Minutemen made their fateful stand in Lexington, Massachusetts, on the road to Concord. The news was everywhere. "Last Wednesday, the 19th of April, the Troops of his *Brittanick* Majesty commenced Hostilities upon the People of this Province," proclaimed the

[1] The narrow, winding foot road called the Wilderness Road remained for years the main route for immigrants over the mountains into Kentucky and, later, to western lands beyond. It wasn't until 1796 that the section over the Cumberland Gap was widened for wagons. Today, U.S. Highway 25-E follows much of the original Wilderness Road route.

Salem Essex Gazette. "We are now involved in all the Horrors of a civil War." There was little chance now that the royal governors would have time or energy to pay attention to what Henderson and his road crew were doing in Kentucky.

Henderson was anxious to have the Wilderness Road ready for the first caravan of settlers. The route would wind more than 250 miles from the Holston River in Tennessee, across the nearby Clinch and Powell rivers, over the Cumberland Gap and Cumberland River northwest into the heart of the bluegrass region, on the banks of the Kentucky River. Where it didn't meander along steep, rocky ridges, the road followed buffalo traces, Indian trails, and streambeds with names like Moccasin and Troublesome Creek. For the backbreaking work of chopping through thick cane, brush, and trees, each road cutter was to receive ten pounds, ten shillings sterling—enough money to purchase about 420 acres of good bluegrass land.

Along with Daniel went his brother Squire and Michael Stoner. Others included Capt. William Twitty (also spelled *Twetty*), his slave, and seven men from North Carolina. One black woman came along on the difficult, dangerous journey. She was a slave belonging to Col. Richard Callaway, Daniel's neighbor from the Yadkin.

The road cutters gathered together at "the Long Island" in the Holston River in what is now Tennessee. On March 10, 1775, work began. The group was full of hope and high spirits. They shared a fine bear for their first meal together. "Every heart abounded with joy and excitement," wrote young Felix Walker, who kept a diary of the trip.

Carelessly, Daniel posted no guards that night or any night for the next two weeks. The men expected no trouble from the Indians. Hadn't they just left the Cherokee ready for a celebration feast?

Daniel and his men cut away miles of thick cane and brush to make a passable track over the Clinch Mountains along the Warrior's Path. They forded the Clinch River and crossed Powell Mountain. They stopped at Martin's Station for supplies, then pushed over the Cumberland Mountains to the Cumberland Gap. The route followed buffalo paths along the Cumberland River. On March 22, they hacked their way through thick cane and reed and suddenly discovered "the pleasing and rapturous appearance of the plains of Kentucky," Walker wrote. "A new sky and strange earth seemed to be presented to our view."

The men who had never been to Kentucky were surprised and excited by the gently rolling bluegrass country. The soil was rich, the fields were covered in fragrant clover, and the forests were filled with wild game.

And then, Kentucky showed the other side of its face.

On the morning of March 25, Shawnee fired into the sleeping camp. Captain Twitty's slave, Sam, was killed. Twitty himself was hit in both knees, fell to the ground, and would have been scalped except that his small bulldog fiercely grabbed hold of an Indian's ankles. By the time the bold dog was tomahawked, Daniel and his men were able to shoot at the attackers and save Twitty's life.

Walker was seriously wounded, but he managed to escape with his scalp by crawling into the underbrush and hiding. Squire had awakened and moved away from the campfire so quickly that he grabbed his jacket instead of his shot pouch. He had to crawl on all fours until he found his brother and could borrow ammunition.

Daniel and the others watched the Indians dart away with their horses and supplies. Badly shaken, they waited for another attack.

The men's nerves were raw. Most expected to be massacred at any moment. The group's enthusiasm for Kentucky had disappeared as quickly as the morning mist. "Hope vanished from the most of us," lamented Walker, whose wounds were so serious that Daniel directed the men to build a crude, temporary shelter for him and Twitty.

On the third morning, as Callaway's slave gathered firewood, she suddenly noticed a pair of eyes in the forest. She screamed as loud as she could for help. Daniel instantly grabbed his rifle and ordered the men to take aim behind trees "and give battle, and not to run till they saw him fall." Tense moments passed. Then they heard a small voice from the forest, the voice of a man who had run off during the attack and had become lost. Sheepishly, he returned to camp. That same day, Twitty died and was buried beside his slave.

Soon afterwards, a half-frozen stranger was discovered in the woods. He told how his nearby camp had also been attacked by the Shawnee; two men had been killed and scalped. To avoid being tracked through the snow and killed, he had run barefoot down an icy stream in the dark.

Boone's men were ready to bolt back to the settlements. They'd seen enough of Kentucky. The most terrified didn't even say farewell. They simply grabbed their guns and a few supplies and went home the way they had come.

But Daniel stubbornly would not retreat. They had come too far. He encouraged the men as best he could. On the morning of April 1, before moving on from their "battleground," he sent a letter by messenger to Henderson, who was supposed to be following them with a wagon train and a group of well-armed men. "Your company is desired greatly, for the people are very uneasy, but are willing to stay and venture their lives with you, and now is the time to flusterate their [the Indians'] intentions and keep the country, whilst we are in it," Daniel pleaded. "If we give way to them now, it will ever be the case."

What Daniel wanted was some kind of sign, some way to convince the others that help was on its way. For twelve days, he waited for Henderson's reply, all the time managing to keep those who remained from running off.

It's easy to imagine the bombshell effect when, on April 7, the messenger reached Henderson and his men camped a hundred miles away in snow near the Cumberland Gap. Henderson's caravan, which included cumbersome wagons, had left ten days after Daniel. The group had been moving at a leisurely pace, improving the road as they went. They had encountered "a turrabel frustration," one traveler wrote, complaining of runaway horses, lost hunters, bad crossings, ugly creeks, poor food, and vicious dogs.

To make matters worse, they kept meeting "a great Maney people turnd Back for fear of the Indians." The news in Daniel's letter made many in Henderson's party panic-stricken. Fear "ran like wildfire," Henderson wrote. Some men in the caravan packed their belongings and left in broad daylight. Others, afraid of being called cowards, hurried home in the dark.

In spite of the danger, Henderson could not convince his followers to stand sentry duty at night. This greatly bothered the orderly Henderson, and he complained that his men "wanted rest more than safety." A good evening supper, Henderson decided, "never failed to put off [the worry of] danger for at least twenty-four hours."[2]

Henderson half-expected to see Daniel's face among the settlers fleeing east. With tears in his eyes, Henderson begged for a volunteer to make the dangerous trip to Daniel's men to tell them help was on its way. No one spoke up. Daniel Boone's men wouldn't last, the doubters told him. The road cutters would leave Daniel before Henderson could join him. Why should someone be killed for nothing? Henderson offered a ten-thousand-acre bribe. Finally, one man agreed to act as messenger on the condition that he'd have a partner.

Again, Henderson appealed to the group. No second man volunteered.

The lone volunteer reluctantly disappeared into the forest, carrying "besides his own enormous load of fearful apprehensions, a considerable burden of my uneasiness," wrote Henderson, who managed to convince those remaining in his caravan to continue moving westward.

The messenger made the trip without any problem and arrived April 17. Daniel and his men, who had rigged a crude litter to carry the wounded Walker between two horses, had made the final twelve miles to the banks of the Kentucky River arriving on the evening of April 1.

[2] Reliable sentries proved to be a practical problem for Daniel as well. Road cutters and, later, settlers were often too exhausted from the manual labor of clearing trees, building homes, and planting crops to stand guard all night.

Their 250-mile expedition had taken just a little more than three weeks.

As a tribute to Daniel Boone, the road cutters named their new Kentucky settlement Boonesborough. Its site was on the south side of the Kentucky River, a level grassy area banked by forest-covered hills. The men watched a herd of nearly three hundred buffalo frolicking near a salt lick, "a sight some of us never saw before, nor perhaps may never again."

It was Walker's good fortune that he had Daniel to nurse him back to health. "He was my father, my physician, and friend," Walker later said. "He attended me as his child, cured my wounds by the use of medicines from the woods." The road cutters chopped trees and hastily erected a handful of cabins. The careless men were in such a hurry to pace off their own plots and throw together their own cabins that they were soon exhausted and refused to stand guard after the first night of their arrival. Three days later, one man was killed by Indians. Even then, the group refused to take seriously their mutual safety. Land hunger was too strong—or maybe they were just too tired.

When Henderson's bedraggled caravan finally peered through the trees on April 20, 1775, they were greeted with a volley of shot from twenty-five guns, every rifle in Boonesborough.

"Although we had nothing here to refresh ourselves with, but cold water and lean buffalo beef, without bread, it certainly was the most joyous banquet I ever saw," wrote careworn Henderson, who nearly collapsed from exhaustion. He was thankful to be alive and could scarcely believe Daniel's men were still alive as well. He later admitted, "It was owing to Boone's confidence in us and the people's in him that a stand was ever attempted in order to wait for our coming."

In 1819, when Daniel was eighty-five, Chester Harding created this portrait, the only one of Daniel known to have been painted from life. Harding used oilcloth because he was unable to find canvas. Forty years later he found the portrait damaged but was able to cut out and save the face.

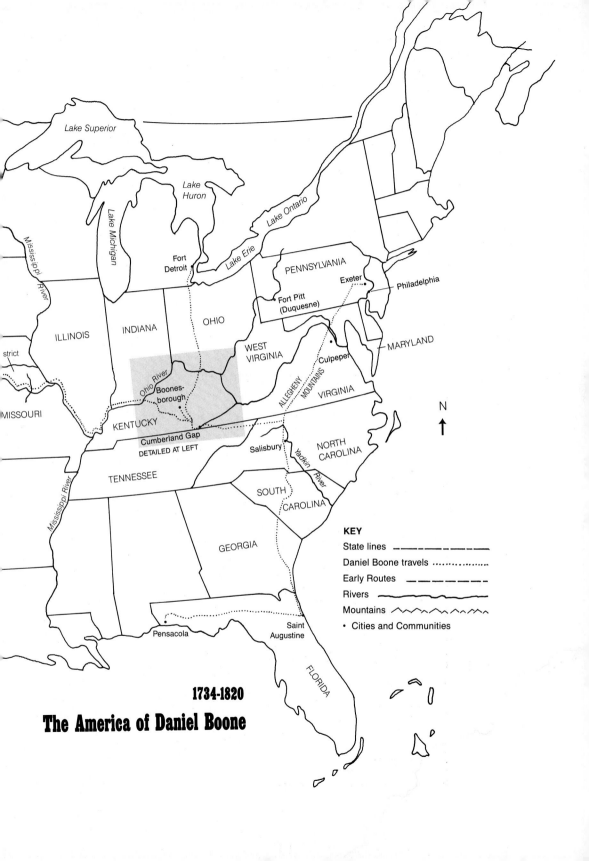

1734-1820

The America of Daniel Boone

Indians surprising Daniel and John Stuart on their Kentucky expedition of 1769.

The interior of the McGinty blockhouse as it probably looked in the 1770s. The blockhouse was rebuilt as part of the 1930s reconstruction of Harrodsburg.

This drawing of Boonesborough was published in *Boonesborough* by George Ranck in 1900 and shows the fort just before the siege of 1778. The drawing is supposed to have been made from Henderson's plans.

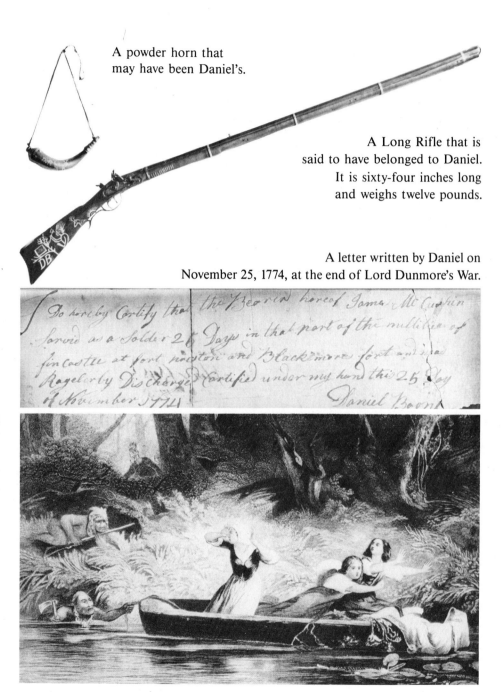

A powder horn that
may have been Daniel's.

A Long Rifle that is
said to have belonged to Daniel.
It is sixty-four inches long
and weighs twelve pounds.

A letter written by Daniel on
November 25, 1774, at the end of Lord Dunmore's War.

A highly romantic 1852 lithograph depicting the capture of Jemima Boone
and the Callaway girls.

A drawing of the Battle of Blue Licks from the 1879 edition of John A. McClung's *Sketches of Western Adventure*.

Daniel surprises the Shawnee in his tobacco shed. This illustration is from Cecil Hartley's *The Life and Times of Colonel Daniel Boone*, published in 1859.

Chapter Eleven

Arrival in a Rich Land

Once the merrymaking of reunion ended, Henderson took a good look at his new settlement that had been named Boonesborough (and not Hendersonville). He did not like what he saw. The few rude cabins that had been built were on low ground, dangerously close to the river. A nearby bluff seemed to leave the settlement open to attack. Everything would have to be moved upriver, Henderson announced.

It's doubtful that anyone paid any attention to him. For a week, everyone seemed oblivious to danger or to practicality of any kind. They were too busy arguing over claims. Because Daniel's men had arrived first, they had taken the liberty of choosing lots of two acres and building their own cabins. Naturally, they picked the best land.

Henderson solved the problem by creating a lottery for everyone, even Daniel's road cutters. This drew complaints. "We all view our loots [sic] & Some Don't like them," one wrote.

The planting season was slipping past quickly. Four lots had to be selected and cleared as soon as possible for the fort garden. Henderson directed the planting. Rolling up his sleeves, he dutifully sowed "small seed, cucumbers & c[orn]." He also tried to smooth the deteriorating tempers of his partners, Luttrell and Hart. They could not agree on the fort's proper site. Hart became so angry that he went off in a sulk and built his cabin away from all the rest.

Every day more travelers arrived on the Wilderness Road. It was amazing how many people suddenly materialized in Kentucky—adventurers, settlers, and land speculators. The arrival of a small group of angry representatives from Harrod's nearby settlement caused some confusion. Harrodsburg had been constructed a year before the Cherokee signed Henderson's treaty. The settlement was within the boundaries of Transylvania. Although it had been temporarily abandoned, Harrodsburg was now populated with fifty young riflemen, mostly without families. Six-foot-tall James Harrod and his notorious bad temper were not to be trifled with. Did Henderson understand Harrod did not intend to give up his claim? After all, wasn't he here first?

With characteristic diplomacy and charm, Henderson managed to soothe everyone's ruffled feathers by promising that Harrodsburg would have equal representation in Transylvania's new government. He sent Harrod away in good humor. Henderson even managed for six weeks to entertain an old friend of Lord Dunmore's—an avowed enemy of the Transylvania Company and a suspected British spy.

With so many "guests," Daniel was having problems finding enough fresh meat for Boonesborough's ever-growing population. Records show as many as 107 men came to live at Boonesborough either temporarily or permanently in 1775. The total number of settlers who took up land throughout Kentucky that first year was said to be nearly five hundred. All needed to eat, even while game was quickly disappearing. At times Daniel had to travel nearly thirty miles to hunt. Wasteful, trigger-happy hunters were partly responsible for the scarcity. "Some would kill three, four or five or ½ a dozen buffalo and not take half a horse load from them all," Henderson wrote.

On May 23, 1775, Henderson held Boonesborough's first meeting in a romantic setting under a lofty giant elm. Invited to participate were delegates chosen to represent Harrodsburg, Boiling Springs, and Logan's

Station. Among the six Boonesborough delegates elected were Daniel Boone, his brother Squire, and Richard Callaway.[1]

The convention beneath the elm lasted four days. It became clear that Henderson did not plan a democratic government for Boonesborough. Civil and military officials would be appointed by Henderson and his partners, not elected by general vote. Settlers must pay unpopular quitrents.

One of the first bills passed by the newly formed government was designed "for preserving game." It was suggested by Daniel, who proposed another "for improving the breed of horses." A rule was passed against "profane swearing and Sabbath breaking."

In spite of his pleasure in the delegates, whom he described in his journal as "very good men and much disposed to serve their country," Henderson was becoming very weary of the hardships of the wilderness. He missed his family. He missed civilization. And his opinion of most of the Boonesborough inhabitants was getting lower by the moment: "a set of scoundrels who scarcely believed in God or fear a devil if we were to judge from most of their looks, words, and actions."[2]

Daniel was also anxious to see his wife and children again. Rebecca was expecting their ninth child. He planned to gather up his family and return with them before snowfall. Squire Boone and Colonel Callaway also planned to bring their families to settle in Kentucky.

---

[1] Almost a week later, on May 28, a visiting minister used the shade of the elm to conduct religious services. Little did the small congregation realize that the minister's prayer for the British royal family would be the first and last said in Kentucky. The next day, the settlers learned by letter that the Revolutionary War had begun.

Although raised a Quaker, Daniel's brother, Squire, had become a Baptist. He would eventually serve as Boonesborough's preacher.

[2] Henderson had other problems as well. In 1775, he petitioned the Continental Congress in Philadelphia that Transylvania be included as the fourteenth colony. At the same time he pledged loyalty to the crown in case George Washington and his fellow rebels lost. The Continental Congress refused the request. John Adams, who thought the Transylvania quitrents unfair, stated, "The [Transylvania Company] partners have no grants from the crown, nor any from any colony, are within the limits of Virginia [and] charged with Utopian Schemes."

On June 13, Daniel headed back to Virginia's Clinch River valley. Left alone to manage the troubles of the unruly Boonesborough residents, Henderson waited impatiently for Daniel's return. The settlers seemed to have faith only in Daniel. "Until [Boone] comes, the devil himself can't drive the others this way," complained Henderson, who was unable to get the settlers to do anything he wanted.

Daniel arrived home in time for the birth of his fifth son, William, on June 20. The baby was sickly and soon died. There was scarcely time to mourn. In less than two months, Daniel and Rebecca set off with their other children: Israel, sixteen; Jemima, thirteen; Lavinia, nine; Rebecca, seven; Daniel Morgan, six; and Jesse, two. Fifteen-year-old Susannah, who had recently married William Hayes, a member of the Wilderness Road crew, may have also journeyed with her parents.[3]

With the Boones and other settlers came twenty young men from North Carolina. The travelers brought supplies of salt, ammunition, and noisy herds of cattle, hogs, ducks, and chickens. Thirty went with Daniel to Boonesborough; the rest went to Harrodsburg.

What did Rebecca think September 8, 1775, as their horses climbed the final ridge overlooking the Kentucky River? Now at last she could see the place that had kept her husband away all those long, lonely days and nights. Daniel must have pointed proudly.

Boonesborough was not much to look at. It consisted of only four or five cabins built along the banks of the Kentucky River. A stockade, or log wall, in a parallelogram shape 260 feet long by 180 feet wide around the cabins was still open on two sides. In the northwest corner was Henderson's house, with a second cabin erected as his kitchen.

[3] One report states that Susannah Boone Hayes had to hurry into Boonesborough because she was pregnant and about to deliver. She gave birth at Boonesborough to a daughter who died in infancy. The next baby born in Boonesborough, whose name was not recorded, was the son of a slave. Susannah's second baby, Elizabeth, was born June 12, 1776, and lived to adulthood. Susannah was one of only a dozen women living at Boonesborough that first year. They included her mother, Rebecca; her sisters; and Rebecca's in-laws.

The air was filled with wood smoke and the barking of dogs. Rebecca could recognize what remained of the cornfields and Henderson's little vegetable patch. But everything else about the place must have seemed lonely and unfamiliar. In all her years of moving with Daniel and the children from one crude cabin to the next, this was as far from civilization as she had ever lived.

Boonesborough teetered on the edge of nowhere, three hundred miles from any real town, real store, real church. The closest settlement was tiny, struggling Harrodsburg. Only the primitive Wilderness Road—an easy place for any Indian ambush—connected Rebecca and her family to the rest of the world. Beyond their new home lay endless forest filled with every kind of danger.

Henderson was not present to greet Daniel when he returned to Boonesborough. He had started on his way back to North Carolina in August 1775 and would not return again for nearly five years. When he arrived in "civilization" again, Henderson and his partners voted to award Daniel his two thousand acres for service to the Transylvania Company.[4]

In Henderson's absence, it became clear that the Boonesborough leadership was on Daniel's shoulders. During the autumn, settlers arrived daily. In September, Squire Boone returned, bringing many of Rebecca's relatives. Colonel Callaway and his family journeyed to Kentucky around the same time, on the way meeting friendly Cherokee who shared buffalo with them. Another welcome arrival was Simon Kenton. Although only twenty years old, he was a respected, experienced rifleman.

One of the first Boonesborough settlers remembered how he rode

[4] Unfortunately, this was land Daniel would never legally own. In June 1776, Virginia declared itself independent of Great Britain. Six months later, on December 7, 1776, the Virginia assembly created the County of Kentucky and incorporated it into the Virginia Commonwealth. In two years, the Transylvania Company was officially dead, complicating land ownership for the first Boonesborough settlers.

Henderson and his partners were awarded a "consolation grant" of 200,000 acres by the Virginia government.

in his mother's lap on horseback. His father rigged seats to carry two small brothers by poking openings in a bed coverlet hung over either side of a packhorse. Eleven-year-old Elizabeth Pogue Thomas and her parents traveled with Colonel Callaway. Her father was "an ingenious contriver," capable of making from wood all kinds of things the pioneers needed—piggins, noggins, and churns.[5] Elizabeth remembered Boonesborough cabins so hastily built near the water's edge that when the Kentucky River rose, "we were afraid it would have entered the cabins."

The first order of business for each new settler was to build a log cabin. Neighbor helped neighbor as logs were lifted and placed in a rectangle, one atop the next, to form four walls. Because there were no metal nails or screws, hardwood maple pegs were used. Cracks between logs were daubed with mud to keep out snow and wind. The chimney and crude fireplace were usually made of stone. The roof was of split oak or cedar clapboards. Bark gutters collected precious soft rain water in homemade, split-wood barrels since there was no well inside the fort yard.

It was damp, dark, and drafty in a Boonesborough cabin. Quarters were often cramped and difficult to keep clean. The floor was hard-packed dirt. There was no glass in the window—if there was a window. The only light came from the fireplace or an open door. "Now fancy yourself a log cabin of the size and form of [a]...dining room—one story high—without a window—with a door opening to the south—with a half-finished wooden chimney—with a roof on one side only—without any upper or lower floor," wrote one man who settled with his parents and three brothers and sisters in Kentucky.

The inside of a Boonesborough cabin was furnished simply. There may have been a wood-slab table and rough hickory chairs with deerskin-slat seats. Perhaps against one wall was a wood bedframe covered with a buffalo skin or a tick stuffed with lumpy corncobs. Iron pots and skillets were the only cooking utensils. Dried, hollow gourds of all

[5] A piggin is a small wooden pail with a long wood strip that serves as a handle. A noggin is a small cup or mug.

shapes and sizes served to carry water and eggs and to store cornmeal, soft soap, even maple sugar. Rifles, powder horns, fishing poles, bundles of dry herbs, strings of red peppers, and maybe a "hand" or two of dry tobacco hung from wooden pegs or buck antlers, which also served as the family's clothes "closet."

In a more well-to-do cabin, like that belonging to Henderson, there could have been a shelf over the fireplace containing a set of shining bowls and trenchers carved from buckeye, a few bottles of medicine, a whiskey jug, a tinder box, an ink bottle and quill pens, and perhaps the Bible, an almanac, *Pilgrim's Progress*, and a volume of Shakespeare.

The fort's palisade was a tall row of pickets, twelve- or sixteen-foot lengths of tree trunk split and sharpened at the top and sunk deeply and firmly into the ground. Crossbeams of wood were used to strengthen these fort "walls." Plans were to build a blockhouse or bastion at each corner. The fort's protection against Indian attacks was certainly neither fire- nor bullet-proof. The wooden walls burned easily, and a shot could find its way between cracks in the logs.

The gate to the fort was so heavy a man alone could barely swing it. Settlers needing to enter or leave propped the gate open with logs.

Animal skins hung on the inside walls of the palisades; pack saddles and iron plows waiting for repair were stacked beside the crude blacksmith shop. Nearby were stock troughs carved from hollow logs. What precious corn and fodder had been harvested was stored in small sheds.

Finding enough food was to be an everlasting problem for Daniel and other early settlers. There was no wheat to make bread. The very little corn that had been harvested or carried from the East was barely enough to go around.

Game kept the settlers from starvation. "I supported the family, mostly with my gun," one settler said. One little boy, like many adults, became quickly tired of eating only meat and more meat. "My parents often told me afterwards," wrote Daniel Drake, who came to Kentucky when he was a toddler, "that I would cry & beg for bread when we were seated round the table till they would have to leave it & cry themselves."

⅄ The settlers had no refrigerators to safely store their buffalo, deer, turkey, and bear meat. Salt was the only preservative. Without it, meat spoiled rapidly. Salt was so crucial to survival that a bushel was worth nearly two cows in barter. In addition to worrying about bringing in enough meat, Daniel also had to concern himself with whether the Boonesborough salt supplies would last through the winter.

There were very few fresh vegetables and little fruit available, except what grew wild. "In December, when at night the family were seated around a warm fire, made blazing bright with pieces of hickory bark— a substitute for candles—...every member was engaged with a dull case knife in scraping and eating a sweet and juicy turnip," remembered one early Kentucky settler who savored the vegetable as if it were an apple. At certain seasons, settlers gathered wild fruit such as pawpaws, plums, hackberries, and winter grapes, "so called because they were too sour to be eaten till they had been sweetened by several severe frosts." Other delicacies from the woods included honey locust pods, walnuts, and hickory nuts.

On December 1, 1775, the Transylvania Company opened its land-office doors to a booming business. Those who had arrived first and had "squatted" on the land now hurried to file on their claims. There were nearly nine hundred land entries, totaling 560,000 acres. All seemed to be going well for the Transylvania Company and for Boonesborough, in spite of frequent arguments over boundaries.

The Shawnee soon realized that the noisy flood of white settlers had come to Kentucky to stay. Just before Christmas, they attacked a man and two boys surveying land across the river from the fort. The Boonesborough settlers heard a shot and a yell and watched in alarm as the man ran back for help with one shoe off. He and the boys had become separated, he reported. There was a shot, and he had seen a couple of Indians.

Where were the boys? Daniel quickly organized a group to pursue the Indians. One boy was never found. The other's scalped body was discovered in a cornfield three miles away.

Daniel urged the settlers not to panic. He had seen Indian raids before, and he was determined to make Kentucky his home. There was a stubborn, clannish group who said they would stay, too, no matter what. However, the majority of Boonesborough residents weren't easily convinced. Ammunition was low and would probably not last until spring. So many fled back to the safety of eastern settlements that by July 1776, only two hundred of the five hundred who had come into Kentucky were left. To make matters worse, early in 1776, Henderson and his partners suddenly decided to raise the price of land from twenty to fifty shillings per one hundred acres. Boonesborough residents were also angered to learn that Henderson and his partners held claim to seventy thousand acres at the Falls of the Ohio, land considered by many to be the best in all Kentucky. This claim had been laid out by Daniel, Squire Boone, and a small group of surveyors.

A petition of grievances against the Transylvania Company was signed by eighty-eight Kentucky settlers, including James Harrod, and sent in April 1776 to the group of delegates who were meeting to form America's new government. Daniel's name was notably absent. He remained loyal to his employer.

Boonesborough had managed to limp through the winter with barely enough supplies and food. Fortunately, there were no more Indian attacks. Spring's slow return meant a welcome change in diet. "The women the first spring we came out," an early Kentucky settler wrote, "would follow their cows to see what they ate, that they might know what greens to get."

As the settlers soon learned, however, the spring "pawpawing" days followed by warmer summer weather meant the beginning of more bloodshed.

Chapter Twelve

Kidnapped!

Still dressed in his best go-to-meeting clothes, Daniel dozed in his cabin. It was a warm afternoon, July 14, 1776. Sabbath ceremonies had just ended when he was shaken awake by a pale and terrified Rebecca.

Her words plunged him into the middle of a nightmare that would last three days.

Neither thirteen-year-old Jemima, fourteen-year-old Fanny Callaway, nor Fanny's sixteen-year-old sister, Betsey, had returned to do their milking chores. When someone went down to the river where they had been paddling, the canoe was spotted empty on the opposite bank. Jemima, whose nickname was "Duck," was a good swimmer. It was doubtful she had drowned. No one thought the girls had just wandered off.

There seemed only one explanation for their disappearance. They had been kidnapped—or worse—by Indians. Just a week earlier, a settler had been scalped on Licking River. And Daniel didn't know that this very day another body would be found farther downstream at Salt Lick.

Daniel leapt for his rifle and ran to the river, still barefoot. All the able-bodied men responded to the alarm that electrified Boonesborough. Betsey's suitor, Samuel Henderson (Richard Henderson's

90

younger brother), came so quickly from shaving that his face was half-soapy stubble. The men gathered on the riverbank, rifles trained on the shadowy trees. No one could be sure how many Indians might be hidden.

It was impossible to cross the deep water without the settlement's only canoe. Daniel picked brave young John Gass to swim across to retrieve the boat, cautioning the other men to keep their guns aimed and ready. No Indians. Yet.

When Gass returned safely with the canoe, five men crossed the river with Daniel to look for clues along the shore. Colonel Callaway and ten men on horseback were instructed to ride downstream to the nearest ford and wait in ambush. Silence and surprise were essential to their mission's success. Daniel knew that the minute the Indians saw the rescuers, they would tomahawk their prisoners—if they had let them live until then.

Daniel's men found the Indians' trail and cautiously followed it for several miles until night came. All the men were still wearing their Sunday pantaloons, not exactly the best clothes for tracking. Daniel had left in such a hurry that he had forgotten even to take moccasins. And they had no food, no extra ammunition or supplies.

Daniel turned to John Gass. "How are you feeling after your swim?"

"Cold," Gass replied.

"Well, here is a worthy way to keep warm." Daniel sent Gass back to Boonesborough to collect jerked venison, bullets, and clothing.

Gass returned, and the group started early the next morning. They came upon the Indians' empty camp, cold campfire, and Betsey's distinctive heel marks, which appeared to have been purposefully dug deep in the soft mud. She was the only one of the captives wearing shoes. There were other signs that meant the girls were still alive. Betsey, Fanny, and Jemima had broken branches and twigs all along the way until their fingers blistered. When they could, they ripped strips of cloth from their skirts and left them behind. A piece of handkerchief embroidered with the name *Callaway* was found.

Unfortunately, beyond the Indians' first camp, the clues became confusing. The Indians had cleverly divided into five groups to slow any pursuers. Rather than wasting critical time, Daniel decided not to fan out and follow each group's path. He felt sure the Indians were headed for Shawnee settlements on the Scioto River. Once they reached the Indian camps, it would be nearly impossible to rescue the girls. For the next thirty-five miles, Daniel guided his men along a northerly course that he was certain ran parallel to that of the kidnappers. With this strategy, he hoped the braves would not detect they were being followed and would eventually become careless.

The Boonesborough men camped again Monday night and pushed on at dawn the next day. Now Daniel cautioned quiet. Ahead was a fork in the Licking River where Daniel was certain the Indians had crossed. He was right. There were fresh moccasin prints along the ground as well as more marks from Betsey's shoes and more broken branches. The water was still muddy. The Boonesborough men picked up more clues—a small snake the Indians had stopped to kill wriggling in the path, the carcass of a freshly killed buffalo.

Ahead, Daniel said, would be another stream. Sure enough, there was. The kidnappers' trail disappeared. The Indians had taken precautions before making camp by walking upstream in the water. He suspected they were probably not far ahead, preparing a meal.

Daniel was right again. Not far away they smelled smoke. The Indians were very near—within earshot. He and his men had to be ready for quick action. Daniel whispered his orders. One group would surround one side of the camp. Another would stay with him. He would fire first, then they would all charge the camp, guns blazing. Any hesitation would give the braves time enough to kill the girls.

The Indians had just started cooking their meal. As Daniel had predicted, they were now apparently less worried about being discovered. From his hiding place, Daniel watched them gather wood, collect water in a kettle, and pierce the buffalo hump with a spit. Against a tree was Betsey; the two younger girls lay with their sad, dirty faces in her lap.

The only sentry had left his rifle behind as he strolled about, lighting his pipe.

Without waiting for Daniel's signal, one of his men fired thirty yards into the camp. He missed. In that instant, the Indians and the rescuers spotted each other. Quickly, John Floyd drew a bead on the sentry and knocked him head over heels into the fire. A blast of shots rang out.

"That's Daddy!" Jemima cried.

"Run, gals, run!" Daniel and his men shouted.

The girls made a dash for the trees. But just as a brave was about to disappear into a nearby canebrake, he turned, whipped out his tomahawk, and hurled it at Betsey, barely missing her head.

"Fall down!" Daniel roared. The girls fell flat on their stomachs in the dirt. A few more knives flew past, none finding their mark. Rifles cracked, and the girls scrambled to their feet again.

Whooping and bellowing, the rescuers rushed the camp. In the confusion, one man lifted his rifle to bring the butt down on what he thought was an Indian—a dusky-faced shape with dark hair wearing ragged leggings and a red bandanna.

"For God's sake, man," Daniel barked, grabbing his arm just in time to save Betsey, "don't kill her now! We've come all this way to save her!"

The Indians dodged into the safety of a thick canebrake. They did not have time to take much with them except one small shotgun. "And being so much elated on recovering the three poor little heart-broken girls, prevented our making any further search," Floyd wrote. Daniel believed that Colonel Callaway and his men would apprehend the braves farther north at the Licking River ford. The next day, Daniel and all of Boonesborough would learn that Colonel Callaway had somehow let the fleeing, unarmed, and wounded Indians escape. Colonel Callaway's hurt pride over his failure did not quickly heal.

In the meantime, the exhausted but happy group of rescuers and former captives started back to the settlement, camping overnight a few miles away. Daniel learned that the girls had been captured by three

Shawnee and two Cherokee. All could speak English fairly well. Included in the group was Chief Hanging Maw, a remarkably tolerant Cherokee captor. This respected leader was on his way to a tribal council meeting.

The Indians had treated Betsey, Fanny, and Jemima with kindness in spite of the girls' irritating efforts to sabotage their kidnapping. At every possible turn, the girls had slowed their captors with complaints and tricks designed to leave behind a clearly marked trail. Blaming an injured foot, Jemima had tumbled to the ground with dramatic screams. Betsey had shredded her linen handkerchief. She had ground her heels into every muddy spot she could find along the way. All the girls had broken branches of nearby underbrush, whining that they needed help pulling themselves along. When the Indians put lame Jemima on a horse to hurry the procession, the girls had unmercifully poked the pony until he threw Jemima again and again, providing additional chances for them to scream for help.

Hanging Maw had asked Jemima, "You Boone's girl?"

"Yes," she replied.

"And they, too?" he asked, pointing to Fanny and Betsey.

"Yes," she lied, hoping the Callaway girls would get better treatment.

"Well, we do pretty good for old Wide Mouth this time," he laughed, using Daniel's Cherokee nickname.

In the end, of course, it was Wide Mouth who did pretty good. Daniel's name and the story of the sensational rescue quickly traveled beyond Boonesborough, all the way back to the East, where colonists fighting England hungered for news of victory of any kind.

In Boonesborough, there was soon cause for more rejoicing—the first wedding in Kentucky! In spite of his half-grizzled appearance at the rescue, Samuel Henderson had won the hand of Betsey Callaway.[1]

Tables were spread with what food could be scrounged together, in-

[1] A little more than a year later, Fanny Callaway married John Holder and Jemima Boone married Flanders Callaway, Colonel Callaway's nephew. Daniel insisted his daughter wait until she was fifteen years old to marry.

cluding "the first homegrown watermelons, of which the whole station was proud." The little whiskey available was raised in toast. And the fort rocked with dancing all night long.

The only unsettling shadow was news brought by a recent visitor. The latest copy of the *Virginia Gazette* told how the colonies had declared their independence from England on July 4, 1776, just two weeks earlier. What did it all mean? The crowd listened, some jubilant, others nervous as the Declaration of Independence was read aloud.

But it is not likely the settlers worried much about their relationship to England. Their most immediate problem had nothing to do with politics—it had to do with plain physical safety.

Life in remote Kentucky was becoming more dangerous by the minute. One settler wrote back East: "The Indians seem determined to break up our settlement, and I really [fear], unless it was possible to give us some assistance, that the greatest part of the people must fall prey to them...Fresh sign of Indian is seen almost every day."

In coming months, the kidnapping would prove to be just the beginning of bad times for Boonesborough.

Chapter Thirteen

Capture
at the Salt Licks

While the Revolutionary War raged along the Atlantic Coast, settlers in Kentucky were isolated and often forgotten by the newly formed Continental Congress. From 1775 until 1782, the settlements faced attack from Indians intent on recapturing their homelands. Tribes were lavishly supported with British guns, artillery, and gifts and reinforced with British soldiers and officers.[1] England viewed her Indian allies as a way to scare into submission the settlers of Kentucky and the Ohio River valley, "the back door to the rebellious colonies."

Supporting the Indians was expensive and a basic misjudgment by the British. Many of the immigrants who came to Kentucky had not formed a definite allegiance to either the American or British side. If the British had protected the Kentucky forts instead of aiding the Indians, they might easily have won the settlers' loyalty.

All of Kentucky was a single large county of Virginia. The revolutionary government in Virginia headed by Patrick Henry may have been sympathetic to the Kentuckians and their struggle with Indians. But there

[1] The Kentuckians had a special name for the British lieutenant governor, Col. Henry Hamilton, stationed in Detroit. They called him the Hair Buyer because he offered the Shawnee bounty payments for American scalps.

simply weren't men or supplies to be spared. In February 1777, Harrodsburg representatives pleaded: "We are surrounded with Enemies... our Fort is already filled with widows and orphans...the apprehension of an invasion...fills our minds with a thousand fears."

⚔ Virginia responded not by sending help but by drafting every able-bodied Kentuckian into military service and making men like Daniel official militia captains and fort commanders. Most Kentucky settlers were fed up. So many fled that by 1777, seven "stations," or clusters of crude, fortified cabins, stood temporarily abandoned. The remaining estimated 150 riflemen and their families crowded into the three strongest forts: Logan's Station, Harrodsburg, and Boonesborough.

The year 1777 was a real test for these Kentucky settlers. Remembered as the Year of the Three Sevens, it was a time of nearly continuous Indian attack. Neither hunting nor farming could be done in any ordinary kind of way. Every movement had to be guarded.

The Indians stole an estimated two hundred of the settlers' horses in twelve months, in addition to killing or scattering cattle. Without horses, speedy communication with the next settlement was almost impossible. Without cattle, malnutrition was likely.

No one knew what "secret mischief" the Indians would do next. One day, only a red cloak hanging out to dry on a clothesline was stolen; another day, a baby was grabbed from its mother's arms and dashed head-first against a tree. Atrocities against the whites were matched with atrocities against the Indians. Some settlers took grisly pride in displaying Indian scalp "trophies" they had taken. At Harrodsburg, the bodies of three dead braves were fed to the dogs "to make them fierce."

People from surrounding farms had to spend many days huddled uncomfortably together in smelly, fly-infested forts without enough food or water. When Josiah Collins reached Boonesborough in December 1777, he was moved to write: "We found a poor distressed, ½ naked, ½ starved people, daily surrounded by the savage."

The stress made some people nearly crazy. Men, women, and children quarreled. Some settlers wandered around the fort "looking and peeping about," hair disheveled, mumbling to themselves.

The confinement was hard on children, who were not allowed to venture into the open alone. Even in the safety of their own beds, they were often warned, "Lie still and go to sleep or the Shawnee will catch you." The fear one settler felt when she was seven years old stayed with her all her life. Sarah Spillman Graham remembered the Sunday she and her brothers and sisters disobeyed their parents and wandered off alone. "A parcel of us had gone off to gather wild cherries and paw-paws; and then came to this sink-hole where there was a spring to drink. The boys saw the [Indian] tracks in the edge of the pond and told us to fly for our lives...The boys were soon out of sight and I was left the last behind and had to guess my way home."

There was also bravery and generosity among those who would not give up on Kentucky. "They was a couragus people but yet I will say they all looked very wild," Daniel Trabue recalled after coming upon the settlers in Logan's Station. "The people...was remarkably kind to us with what they had, but I thought it was hard times, no bread, no vegetables, no fruit of any kind, and no ardent spirits."

After surviving an unusually long, cold winter, Boonesborough faced more Indian attacks in the spring. In April 1777, two men went down to the river to collect firewood and find out why the cows were acting so frightened. Daniel ordered his scout, Simon Kenton, to stand at the fort gate and cover for the men. But as the two started back with their arms full, they were met with a barrage of shots. One man was hit.

Six Indians rushed from the woods, tomahawked the wounded settler, and fled. A dozen riflemen led by Daniel emerged from the fort in chase. They stopped suddenly, sixty yards from the gate, as Shawnee Chief Blackfish and fifty warriors burst into view behind them, cutting off their escape.

Daniel yelled to the men to charge through the Indians. "Boys, we'll have to fight for it—sell your lives dear!"

After a single volley of shots, there was no time to reload. Raising their guns over their heads like clubs, the settlers met the Indians in hand-to-hand combat. A Shawnee took a shot at Daniel and shattered his anklebone. As he dropped to the ground, another warrior was on top of him, ready to take his scalp.

A rifle cracked. The Indian slumped. Strapping twenty-two-year-old Simon Kenton, agile enough to load on the run, had shot the attacker through the chest. When another Indian went for Daniel's scalp, Kenton hit him in the head with the butt of his rifle.

With his free arm, he picked up Daniel and ran toward the fort. Jemima saw him and ran to help carry her father. The gate shut with everyone inside. There had been one man killed, seven wounded.

As Daniel was taken to his bed, he turned to thank Kenton. "Well, Simon, you behaved like a man today. You are a fine fellow."

The Shawnee gave up and rode away, but everyone knew they would return. There was much to do before the next attack. Food and fresh water were running dangerously low. While Daniel was laid up in bed for several weeks, he ordered that the fort walls be strengthened and corn planted and cultivated. A well needed to be dug inside the fort walls to provide water in case of a long siege.[2]

A month later, the Indians returned, firing on the fort a full day. When they did not succeed, they made another attack July 4 with a war party of two hundred braves. For two days, the Shawnee burned and destroyed cabins and crops outside the fort. Throughout the attack, which left one settler dead, Daniel hobbled about with help from a walking stick, directing the defense. Boonesborough did not fall.

Now ammunition was nearly gone. The settlers considered making the dangerous trip to Logan's Station or Harrodsburg to borrow needed powder and lead. Someone remembered a small amount of brimstone

[2] All fort drinking water came from rain barrels or a spring some distance away. Unfortunately, when digging became too difficult, the settlers gave up and the half-finished well was abandoned.

and saltpeter hidden among Henderson's supplies. Daniel and the men made charcoal and mixed their own gunpowder, enough to last a little while longer, while the women melted pewter plates for bullets.[3]

Rumors had spread east that Daniel was seriously wounded and all Kentuckians were under siege. At last there was a response. On August 1, Col. John Bowman arrived with one hundred Virginia militiamen. Maj. William Bailey Smith called together forty-eight volunteers—mostly Daniel's friends and kinfolk from the Yadkin valley—and marched them through the Boonesborough gates on September 13. When Blackfish heard mistakenly from his scouts that reinforcements numbered more than two hundred, he changed his plans for attacking immediately.

The armed volunteers brought hope and the first red, white, and blue American flag with thirteen stars seen west of the mountains. But the militia and Smith's men were on short-term enlistments and stayed only long enough to provide protection while the settlers harvested what little remained of their crops.

In late autumn, Shawnee Chief Cornstalk and his son were shot in cold blood by soldiers during peace negotiations at Fort Randolph near Point Pleasant, Virginia. The Shawnee, led by Chief Blackfish, were outraged at the murder of their powerful leader, who had tried to act as a friend to whites. With support from the British, they prepared to mount a massive attack. The war campaign in winter was unusual; ordinarily, the Shawnee preferred fighting in warmer weather.

Unaware and unprepared, Kentuckians huddled in forts. The winter countryside was strewn with abandoned homes, abandoned fields, abandoned dreams. An eighteen-year-old militiaman on his first trip to Kentucky later remembered marching cheerfully with a small group of fellow soldiers as far as the Powell River valley, east of the Cumberland Gap.

---

[3] During attacks at Boonesborough and the other two remaining stations, women often took turns shooting from fort loopholes, which were narrow slits in the fort walls. They also helped load powder and lead and cared for the wounded—in addition to their regular duties of cooking, washing, and watching the children.

There, they were shocked to discover large-scale destruction in the wake of fleeing Kentuckians. "Seeing vast Desolate Cabbins I began to feel strange," he wrote. "I was afraid I should be killed in this Drary howling Wilderness but I never mentioned it to anyone."

As Daniel looked toward the new year, he saw nothing but problems. Fortifications were still not complete; gaps stood between some palisade logs. There was no well, and blockhouses had been built only in two corners. Daniel and the other fort commanders could not convince weary settlers to put their backs to the reinforcement work during infrequent lulls of peace. The food supply was again running dangerously low, and the salt supply—so necessary to the preservation of meat and the curing of hides—was rapidly shrinking.

Perhaps, at least, the salt problem could be solved. Daniel knew that in the surrounding limestone country were many hidden underground springs of salt water, trapped between layers of rock and sand. The water bubbled up through the surface at certain places, creating salt- and sulphur-encrusted springs. These "licks," as they were called, attracted salt-hungry deer and buffalo. The nearest one, Lower Blue Licks, was forty miles north on the Licking River.

In the dead of winter, Daniel thought, the Indians would cause no trouble. He knew most spent the cold months camped in villages along the Scioto River. In early January 1778, Daniel organized a company of thirty men, the best shots from three stations. Heavy salt kettles, which had been gifts from the Virginia government, were strapped to packhorses. The men would serve a one-month shift, then be replaced by another team of workers until a year's worth of salt was collected.

Collecting salt was hard work. Nearly 840 gallons of briny water had to be boiled down to produce just one bushel of salt. Wood had to be chopped and fires fed.

Three scouts kept constant watch in the nearby forest; for several weeks, there were no signs of Indians. More than three hundred bushels of salt were sent back on packhorses to the settlements, and the next team of workers was expected soon. The men were feeling confident. For once, luck seemed to be smiling on the Kentuckians.

Throughout a cold February 7, Daniel hunted, scouted, and checked his beaver-trap lines. As he returned to the salt camp at nightfall with a freshly killed buffalo, he was caught in a surprise snowstorm. In the quiet of the snowy forest, he sensed something following him. An animal? He turned. Four Indians were gaining on him rapidly.

He knew he could not fight off four men at once. Perhaps if he cut the heavy buffalo from his horse, he might be able to jump on and escape.

But when Daniel pulled his knife to cut off the carcass, he discovered that buffalo grease had frozen the blade inside the sheath. He abandoned his horse and started to run through the snow. Warning shots were fired. There was no escape. Daniel leaned his rifle against a tree and approached the Indians, making a sign of surrender.

The Shawnee took him to their camp, an hour's walk away. There he was shocked to discover Chief Blackfish's impressive war party— more than one hundred painted braves equipped and directed by a handful of British soldiers. Many Indians recognized the well-known Long Knife.[4] Even short, sturdy Chief Blackfish, the famous war chief, rose to shake hands.

Daniel quickly learned that the Indians planned to revenge Chief Cornstalk's death by crushing Boonesborough and then sweeping through Harrodsburg and Logan's Station. The men would be killed and scalped; the women and children would be taken prisoners.

Daniel had to think quickly while at the same time revealing no concern. He knew that the defenses of all three Kentucky forts were weak. The best riflemen from Boonesborough, Harrodsburg, and Logan's Station were in the salt camp or in the relief team, on its way.

"How d'y, Captain Will," Daniel said good-naturedly, shaking hands with the Indian he had met on his first trip to Kentucky. "You steal my

---

[4] Long Knife was a name thought to have been given by the Indians to white hunters because many carried long hunting knives.

horses, remember? You put a bell around my neck. But then I run away, right?"

Captain Will remembered. He laughed, "Boone, you not run away this time!"

When questioned, Daniel lied and said there were more than thirty riflemen at the salt licks and twice that number at Boonesborough. He tried to convince Blackfish that the men who killed Chief Cornstalk were not Kentuckians. The Kentucky settlers, Daniel said, wanted only peace with the Shawnee.

"Cornstalk will not rest until we take revenge," insisted Chief Blackfish through his interpreter, an escaped slave named Pompey.

Daniel tried another tactic. What if the Indians took an impressive number of prisoners? Wouldn't that be just as good, especially if the British in Detroit were willing to pay nearly twenty pounds for each one? He told Blackfish he would lead the Shawnee to the licks and surrender all his best hunters if the Indians would promise not to make them run the gauntlet.[5]

Blackfish paused to consider.

And, Daniel promised, in the spring when the weather was warm and travel with women and children was easier, he would lead Blackfish's braves back to Boonesborough to capture all settlers who remained there. He was certain they would surrender without a fight and go willingly with the Shawnee north to their villages.

Blackfish put out his hand to shake on the bargain that promised much glory and a swift end to an uncomfortable winter campaign. His parting warning to Daniel, however, was that if there was any shooting by the salt makers, the first scalp taken would be Daniel's.

---

[5] The gauntlet was a kind of "greeting" performed mostly for the entertainment of Indians. When prisoners were taken, an entire village, including women and children, would turn out with antlers, bats, poles, sticks, and rocks and stand in two lines. The prisoners had to run between the lines, from one end to the other. Those not bold or strong enough to run quickly were sometimes beaten to death. Those who survived were often adopted by the tribe.

The next day, Daniel and a company of Shawnee left for the salt licks. Through lightly falling snow, Daniel walked into camp ahead of two warriors, calling, "Don't fire or we will all be massacred!"

The Kentuckians froze in their tracks. They listened in disbelief as Daniel explained the deal he had made with Blackfish. He told his men to stack their guns and promised that the Indians would treat them well. The captives would not be made to run the gauntlet. But if they resisted, there would be bloodshed.

The warriors surrounded the salt makers. Suddenly, a young brave demanded all the white men be killed right then and there. Wasn't Cornstalk's death the reason they had assembled this war party? Send this Boone fellow to the white fort. Make the settlers there surrender and then kill them, too.

Daniel must have tried hard not to show his fear. At any moment, he expected the arrival of the unsuspecting relief party—would they be captured, too? He pleaded with Blackfish. The chief decided to hold a council meeting. Those who said the prisoners must die were to pound the war club on the ground; those who said they could live were to pass the war club on.

Arguing continued for hours before the final vote. Daniel had his chance to make an eloquent, moving speech, translated into Shawnee by Pompey and recorded years later by one of the salt makers:

"Brothers!...You have got all the young men; to kill them, as has been suggested, would displease the Great Spirit, and you could not expect success, either in hunting nor war; and if you spare them they will make you fine warriors, and excellent hunters to kill game for your squaws and children. These young men have done you no harm; they were engaged in a peaceful occupation, and unresistingly surrendered upon my assurance that such a course was the only safe one...spare them, and the Great Spirit will smile upon you."

The vote was dangerously close: fifty-nine for death, sixty-one for life. One story says that Chief Blackfish, who had made up his mind to have Daniel as an adopted son, allowed the famous Long Knife to vote. Whether he voted or not, Daniel must have breathed a sigh of relief at the final tally.

His anxiety returned, however, when the British officers who were directing the Shawnee urged them to push on and capture the settlements. Chief Blackfish refused. He said he had all the prisoners he wanted for now. And what about all those riflemen at the Boonesborough stronghold Daniel warned about? Enough was enough.

The Shawnee threw the hard-earned bushels of salt into the snow and took the Kentuckians' horses, guns, and kettles. The Shawnee and their captives began the long, miserable journey back to the Indians' winter camp.[6]

All week long, the white prisoners shuffled through the drifts, wondering if they would ever see their families again. And what had happened to Daniel, the man they had always known and trusted? Many grumbled that their leader had turned into a cowardly traitor.

Daniel, of course, was watched closely by the Indians. He could not let his men know what he was thinking. The first night he had to be even more careful to keep his feelings to himself. After they had made camp, a group of smiling, joking Indians stomped down a hundred-yard path in the snow. Daniel tried not to act disturbed even though he knew what they were making: the warriors' gauntlet.

When Daniel reminded Chief Blackfish of his promise, the chief was said to have replied, "O Captain Boone, this is not intended for your men but for you."

Daniel had no choice. Two rows of braves armed with clubs, switches, and tomahawks were waiting, six feet apart. Stripped to the waist, Daniel rushed zigzag between them with his head down. He butted full in the chest and ran over one imposing brave who stood in his way. Breathlessly, he made it to the end of the line. The admiring Shawnee laughed and cheered. This Daniel Boone would make Blackfish a good adopted son.

---

[6] Late that afternoon, two scouts, Flanders Callaway, Daniel's new son-in-law, and Thomas Brooks, returned to the deserted salt camp. They galloped back to warn Boonesborough.

On February 18, 1778, Blackfish and the captives arrived at Little Chillicothe, the largest Shawnee village, located on the Little Miami river. The chief's arrival was triumphant. He had taken the most prisoners and booty since Braddock had been defeated more than twenty years before. The crowd was so wild with enthusiasm that Blackfish had to break his promise. He made Daniel's men run the gauntlet.

Sixteen captives were adopted by the tribe. The "no goods," those who weren't thought worth adopting, were taken a month later to Fort Detroit, to be sold to the British. Making the trip were ten captives and Daniel, although Blackfish had no intention of selling him. He was taken along to be shown off by the proud Blackfish and his warriors, who now demanded the British pay them for their hard work.

Daniel watched for an opportunity to trick the British into at least stalling their attack of the Kentucky settlements. When asked, he exaggerated Boonesborough's strength. Lt. Gov. Henry Hamilton was fooled. What other helpful information could Daniel Boone provide? Were the Kentucky settlers loyal to the American rebellion?

Daniel smiled. He hinted that perhaps the settlers might be moved to change sides if it were to their advantage.

Daniel's fellow prisoners, who may have heard about this conversation, took it to heart. They mistook Daniel's ruse for yellow-bellied treason. Daniel Boone was no better than that British Hair Buyer, they whispered among themselves.

Lieutenant Governor Hamilton thought well of Daniel. Hamilton tried to purchase him from Blackfish for the very high price of one hundred pounds sterling. Perhaps he hoped Daniel would become a British agent. Blackfish refused, saying he "loved Boone too strongly." But Daniel did not refuse Hamilton's presents. Among other things, he received a fine horse and saddle—gifts which made the other captives envious and more suspicious.

Chapter Fourteen

Sheltowee

That spring, after touring Delaware, Mingo, and Shawnee villages, Daniel and the other prisoners who had not been sold to the British returned to Little Chillicothe. They quickly learned of the escape of Andrew Johnson, one of the adopted prisoners. Clumsy, comical "Little-Shut-His-Eyes," as he was called by the Shawnee because of his poor aim, had stolen a rifle and disappeared. The other captives whispered hopefully about Johnson's chances of making it to safety. All except Daniel—he showed no interest in such talk.

To the disgust of the other prisoners, Daniel seemed to *enjoy* living with the Indians. He hunted and practiced target shooting with the braves. He repaired their guns. He sang and told jokes. Blackfish decided the time was right for an adoption ceremony. Daniel would be his new son.

Except for a four-inch "scalp lock," every hair was painfully plucked from Daniel's head. At the river, he was scrubbed raw from head to foot "to take all his white blood out." Then he was brought to the council house, where his head and face were painted with the tribe's symbols and he was presented with a tomahawk, additional Indian clothes, and a new name, *Sheltowee*, meaning "Big Turtle." When the ceremony was over, the warriors smoked the pipe with their new brother. Everyone feasted on venison, bear fat, corn, and maple sugar.

For four months, from the time he was captured, Daniel carefully built up Blackfish's confidence that he would not try to escape. While the rest of the captives disliked life among the Shawnee, calling them "a parcel of dirty Indians," Daniel seemed content—even happy. And why not? He received special treatment as the chief's adopted son. He did not have to do any hard manual labor like the other whites. The captives later reported that Blackfish even gave his new son a Shawnee girl for his wife.

Sheltowee was doing what he had always loved best, spending spring days hunting and fishing. He felt a genuine fondness for the people who so openly admired him. He later looked back on this time of his life and wrote, "I had a great share in the affection of my new parents, brothers, sisters, and friends." At the same time, Daniel worried. His wife and family and friends were all still at Boonesborough.

The attack that Blackfish planned would come soon. The Shawnee chief still did not entirely trust his adopted son. There were eyes on Sheltowee whenever he grazed his horse or strolled in the long grass, singing at the top of his lungs. A Shawnee companion went with him during hunts to keep track of how much lead and powder he used. As always, Daniel was careful not to incite envy by shooting better than his Shawnee brothers during target matches.

Daniel kept up a relaxed facade. Escape was something he even joked about with the other warriors, who brought him their guns to repair. According to one story, he once played a bold trick on them. He removed all the bullets from their rifles, then announced to his adopted father that he was running away.

"No you ain't," Blackfish replied. "If you attempt it, I'll shoot you."

Sheltowee seemed serious. There he was, about to disappear between the trees. The Shawnee raised their rifles and fired. Their white brother jumped up into the air unhurt, pretending to catch bullets he actually held in his own leather apron.

"Here, take your bullets—Boone ain't going away," he told the astonished braves. When they realized the trick, they rolled on the ground with laughter. That Sheltowee, such a joker!

At every opportunity, Daniel pocketed extra bullets and hid a supply of dried venison. Secretly preparing his escape took time and cunning. He could not show his hand too soon. His exit would have to be perfectly timed or he would jeopardize the lives of the Kentucky settlers. He did not dare confide in any of the other captives.

In June, Daniel learned grim news. A Shawnee war party from another tribe came into camp and told how they had been defeated in western Virginia. An angry Blackfish announced he'd wait no longer to revenge on Boonesborough. The Indians began making plans for the postponed attack.

On June 16, 1778, while the rest of the warriors were off hunting, Sheltowee took his gun, bullets, and a small supply of venison and galloped away, leaving behind his disappointed adopted mother and a group of screaming women.

They sent out the alarm. Sheltowee had fled! Sorrowfully, Blackfish realized his son would go "straight as a leather thong" back to Boonesborough. A runner was sent to Detroit to tell the British that the surprise attack on the Kentucky settlements would have to wait. Sheltowee would warn the settlers to begin their defense.

In less than four days, forty-three-year-old Daniel raced through 160 miles of dense wilderness, all the time expertly confusing any would-be Indian trackers. His exhausted horse gave out after galloping nonstop for a day and night. Daniel let him go free and made the rest of the amazing journey on foot, not stopping to rest or eat. Some accounts say he walked in streams and swung across ravines on grapevines to break his trail.

When he reached the cold, swift Ohio River, he may have crossed with his clothes, gun, and powder on top of a makeshift raft of vine and fallen logs. Daniel pushed on until he was forty miles from home. There he stopped to kill a buffalo. He took the tongue home with him as it was a favorite treat of his eight-year-old son, Daniel Morgan.

Exhausted and gaunt, Daniel, with his scalp lock and Indian clothes, finally staggered through the gate of a strangely deserted Boonesborough. "Daniel Boone. By God. By God!" was all one old friend could say, scarcely believing his eyes.

And where was Rebecca? Where was his family? Daniel demanded.

Gone. They had given up hope that he was still alive and had returned to Rebecca's relatives in North Carolina. Only Jemima and her husband, Daniel's brother Squire, and Squire's family had stayed. The wives and children of the twenty-seven other captured men had also gone back east.

Sadly, Daniel carried the special treat he had brought for Daniel Morgan to his cabin—empty, except for the family's cat, who rubbed its back against his leg.

Would he go back to North Carolina for his family? asked the people of Boonesborough, who looked to Daniel as their natural leader.

No, Daniel replied slowly. He would not abandon them. Before summer was over, there would be an attack, the worst Boonesborough had seen yet. There was much to do to get ready. The stockade was rotted and needed to be repaired. There were gaps between cabins. The gates sagged, and both blockhouses were full of holes. The well had still not been finished.

In Daniel's absence, it had never been clear who was in charge. Although the unpopular Colonel Callaway had struggled without success to take over, Maj. William Bailey Smith was officially in command. Colonel Callaway was unhappy about the situation. The people were badly demoralized, divided, and disorganized.

On July 17, William Hancock, one of the salt makers who had been taken captive, stumbled ragged and half-dead into Boonesborough.[1]

---

[1] Half of the men captured at the salt licks eventually escaped. Two were killed. While a few chose to stay with the British in Canada, the rest came home to Kentucky when the Revolutionary War was over.

Nine days earlier, he had managed to escape from Blackfish's camp with only a handful of parched corn. As Daniel nursed him back to health with broth and hot poultices, he learned that the attack had been delayed for a time because Blackfish had lost heart. But when British officers brought gifts and promises of more, the Shawnee decided to strike at the end of July. This time they'd have four hundred men and four British cannons. If Boonesborough didn't surrender, they'd blow it to bits.

How could the tiny garrison ever manage to survive? The panicked settlers argued about what they should do. Finally, Daniel spoke up. Calmly, he announced he was willing to stay and die with the rest of them if they would work and make a fight of it.

The people of Boonesborough repaired the gate and the stockade between cabins. Two blockhouses were strengthened, and two more were added. Now there was one at each corner of the fort. Food was gathered and stored, and water collected in buckets, pails, and kettles. Bullets were molded, rifles cleaned. Lookouts were posted, and Daniel sent scouts into the woods to patrol for signs of Indians. He called upon the two other remaining Kentucky settlements for support. Logan's Station sent fifteen men and Harrodsburg another five, even though it meant that their own rifle power was reduced. A rider was sent to the Holston River settlements to beg for help from the militia there.

The fort's defenders were nowhere as numerous as Daniel had told Blackfish and Hamilton. There were just fifty riflemen at Boonesborough, including a few young boys who had come as packhorse drivers and stayed.

The fortifications weren't perfect. But they were better than they ever had been. Somehow, hearing Daniel say all their work "would give account of itself" encouraged the settlers. Maybe they had a chance. Just maybe.

"We are all in fine Spirits. . ." Daniel wrote to the Virginia military authorities, pleading for reinforcements, "and intend to fight—hard."

Chapter Fifteen

The Siege
of Boonesborough

By late August, the Indians still had not attacked. The settlers waited. Finally, Daniel decided he'd mount a first-strike force of his own. He hoped to catch the Indians off guard, damage their defenses, and perhaps find out something about their plans. Callaway argued the idea was foolhardy. Others whispered strange stories they'd heard from William Hancock about Sheltowee at the Shawnee camp. Could Daniel Boone be trusted?

In the end, twenty volunteers decided he could. They set out with Daniel, thinking they'd spy on the Indians and maybe take a few furs and horses. But when the group reached the Licking River and realized Daniel meant to push north beyond the Ohio River to the Scioto Valley, the faint-hearted turned back. Daniel intended to take prisoners if he could. Was he crazy? Twenty men could never take on an entire Shawnee nation. A third returned to the fort.

Bravely, Daniel led his scouts, including Simon Kenton, across the Ohio. They raided horses from several villages, sending the Indians into a panic. When Simon Kenton stumbled onto an armed war party, Daniel had a chance to repay his friend for saving his life a year earlier. Daniel's gunfire helped to drive off two Indians who tried to ambush Kenton.

Daniel was alarmed by reports that no warriors were spied in villages along Paint Creek. Blackfish's attack force must already be on the move. Daniel hurried his men back to Boonesborough, leaving Kenton behind to continue scouting. There was no time to lose. On the way past Lower Blue Licks, Daniel came upon an enormous war party of Indians and British, with a train of packhorses.

Daniel could not get close enough to see that at that very moment, the Indians were decorating themselves with some of the 550 pounds of vermillion and 80 pounds of rose-pink war paint that had been given to them by the British army. Loaded on the war party's packhorses, according to Lieutenant Governor Hamilton's August inventory, were ammunition and a sinister supply of "150 dozen scalping knives"—more than Blackfish's band could ever use at one time.

The sight of the war party was enough. Daniel and his men dashed back to Boonesborough, arriving September 6. Everyone in the fort immediately went on alert, measuring gunpowder, cleaning rifles, gathering wood and food, and filling jugs from the spring. Each rifleman was given a position at fort wall loopholes. A woman was stationed next to every rifleman to reload rifles with bullets and powder.

The next morning, Squire's young sons, Moses and Isaiah, were watering horses when they spotted a line of brightly painted warriors on the ridge along the river. With British flags flying, the war party rode straight for Boonesborough's gate. There were more than four hundred Shawnee, Mingo, Wyandot, and Cherokee warriors, and forty-four British officers and soldiers—the largest force ever sent against a Kentucky settlement.

Daniel called to the boys, who ran inside the fort. Women, girls, young boys, and slaves—everyone who had not been assigned to firing stations—put on beaver hats and marched beside the palisade holding up rifles or what looked like rifles. The trick was to make the Indians think there were at least a hundred armed men inside the fort. Smoke rose peacefully from chimneys. Daniel kept the gate partially open to show how confident he was of Boonesborough's defenses.

Blackfish's interpreter, the black man named Pompey, rode with a white flag of truce to the gate. He shouted for Daniel, who made him call again before he finally answered. What did he want? Daniel asked.

Blackfish had letters from Lieutenant Governor Hamilton and wanted them delivered, Pompey said.

Tell Blackfish himself to bring the letters, Daniel replied, biding his time.

Now Blackfish rode to the fort, calling to Sheltowee, his adopted son, to come out. A blanket was spread on the ground for their parley.

The worried men inside Boonesborough told Daniel not to go. They were afraid he'd be made captive again. Daniel said he must meet Blackfish. Every rifleman was ordered to train his sights in Daniel's direction. If he were surrounded and taken prisoner, the gate was to be slammed tight and they were to begin firing.

"How d'y, Boone, how d'y," Blackfish said, shaking hands.

"How d'y, Blackfish."

"Well, Boone, what made you run away from me?"

"It was because I wanted to see my wife and children so bad."

"But you didn't need to run away. If you had let me know, I would have let you come here."

Blackfish gestured toward his army of warriors. He handed Daniel a letter from the British governor urging the settlers to give up and reminding them that the Indians, once a massacre began, would be difficult to control. Blackfish said, "Well, Boone, I have come to take your fort. If you will surrender, I will take you up to Chillicothe and you will be treated well. If not, I will put all the other people to death and reserve the young squaws for myself."

Daniel tried to explain that since he had been gone so long in the Shawnee camp, his people had been given a new chief. "The great Virginia father has sent us a bigger captain here, and he does not want to surrender," Daniel said, referring to Major Smith, who had come to Boonesborough with reinforcements during the terrible Year of the Three Sevens. Daniel promised to try to persuade "the bigger captain."

Major Smith came out for the Indians to see. Posing majestically outside the fort, he looked very much like a commander. His gold-braided, brilliant red militia uniform glittered in the sunlight; the ostrich plume on his hat fluttered in the wind. The Indians seemed impressed.

The old chief told Daniel that his men were very hungry and had nothing to eat. Daniel understood his request immediately. If he did not present the Indians with the food they wanted, Blackfish would realize how poorly supplied the fort was. "There you see plenty of cattle and corn," Daniel said, waving toward the nearby field. "Take what you need, but don't let any be wasted."

While the Indians shot cattle outside the fort, Daniel went back inside to tell the others the bad news. If they surrendered and left their homes, Hamilton might take them in as British subjects. If the settlers fought and lost, the Indians would take no prisoners. Daniel didn't need to explain. Everyone in Boonesborough knew very well that those who managed to survive the attack would be tortured, then scalped.

There were only thirty men, twenty boys, and a few women and children against more than four hundred well-armed warriors. What was the decision?

Daniel's brother, Squire, and his friends Smith, Callaway, Gass, and Holder spoke in favor of resistance. How could they be guaranteed that as the Indians' prisoners they wouldn't be killed before they reached Chillicothe? Squire vowed "he'd fight till he died."

Daniel repeated that Lieutenant Governor Hamilton and the British might treat the settlers fairly *if* they gave up the fort, went to Detroit, and became loyal subjects of the king.

No one argued for surrender. Who could trust the notorious Hair Buyer? The vote of all the men present was unanimous: they would fight to the end.

"Well, then I'll die with the rest," Daniel replied.

For the next two days, a truce was called. All of Boonesborough prayed the delay would allow the Virginia militia and Holston River valley reinforcements time to arrive. Meanwhile, Daniel and Major Smith negotiated as slowly as possible with Blackfish, who presented them with seven roasted buffalo tongues as a token of good faith. Also at the negotiations was a French-Canadian lieutenant in the British Army named Dagneux de Quindre, his white aides, an interpreter, and the powerful, disgruntled Shawnee chief Moluntha. None carried arms. They sat under a shady arbor constructed from branches and blankets, located within sight of the fort.

During these tense rounds of talks, the people in Boonesborough tried to go on with their lives as normally as possible, all the time preparing for the siege they knew must come.

On September 9, some of the braves called out that they wanted to see Sheltowee's famous daughter, the one they had heard so much about from Hanging Maw. Could the famous kidnapped girl come out?

Again, the people of Boonesborough were afraid a captive would be taken. But Daniel ordered the gates opened. The braves were delighted to see Jemima standing nervously with her husband, who carefully eyed the crowd with his rifle loaded.

Could they shake her hand? the Indians asked.

Jemima's husband shook his head. If anyone touched her, he said, he'd kill him. The gates were closed. The Indians went away.

That evening it was Blackfish and de Quindre who came to the fort to demand the settlers' final decision.

"The people are determined to defend the fort while a man is living," Daniel told them.

Blackfish's face fell. He had hoped he would be able to impress the other chiefs with his power by making his adopted son do as he wished.

Another peace talk was suggested by de Quindre. The white officer told Daniel that he and his allies would meet with nine Boonesborough men the next day to draw up a treaty. The terms sounded too good to be true: the warriors would return to their villages, and forevermore there would be peace between the Indians and settlers. Daniel was not

convinced. His adopted father's stern face revealed nothing. Reluctantly, Daniel agreed to meet.

The next day, a proper cloth-covered table was set up near Lick
Spring, only eighty yards from the fort. A clerk wrote down what the
English, Indians, and Americans discussed. Only eight Kentuckians could
be spared from defending the fort. They were Daniel and Major Smith;
Callaway; Daniel's brother, Squire, and son-in-law, Flanders Callaway;
William Buchanan; Stephen Hancock; and William Hancock.

Throughout the negotiations, the hat trick was tried again. Every
man, woman, and child in the fort paraded near the stockade walls in
men's hats. They marched with hats on upraised hands, hats on dum-
mies, hats on broomsticks—all to give the impression that an entire regi-
ment was on guard.

After much courteous discussion and sampling of tasty delicacies
that came all the way from Detroit, an agreement was drawn up to be
signed the next day. Blackfish insisted that during the ceremony he be
accompanied by eighteen young, strong braves. When asked why, he
replied that each would represent one of eighteen tribes. Daniel's sus-
picions grew. He did not believe that Blackfish would go back to his
people empty-handed. It would be too humiliating. But he agreed to
the presence of the eighteen braves, although he insisted the signing must
be made within a rifle's shot of the fort.

The Boonesborough negotiators must have had a sleepless night. They
knew that they'd be outnumbered by more than two to one at the meeting
in the morning. Anxiously they listened while the Indians danced a war
dance—certainly an odd way to prepare for the signing of a peace treaty.

The next morning, September 11, 1778, Daniel ordered twenty-five
of his best marksmen to point loaded rifles at the treaty-signing area.
If trouble started, they were to fire "into the lump."

Unarmed Indians and British gathered, bright and cheerful. Again
the settlers were asked to leave the fort and Kentucky. Again they refused. Then Blackfish surprised everyone by suggesting the Ohio River

be used as a boundary between Indians and settlers. Both must promise not to steal each other's horses. All the settlers had to do was sign an oath of allegiance to the British and submit to Hamilton's authority. How did that sound?

Every one of the eight Boonesborough representatives quickly put quill to ink and signed his name.

"Then we shall live as brothers," Blackfish announced in a resounding voice, "and this treaty shall bind us both as long as the trees grow and water runs in the Kentucky River."

What happened next may never be completely known. After the last puff on the peace pipe, Blackfish announced it was time for "shaking long hands and drawing hearts close" to symbolize friendship. Two warriors grasped the hand of each settler present.

Was it treachery? Panic? Whatever the cause, a scuffle broke out, perhaps as the Boonesborough men tried to squirm free from the warriors' bear hugs.

Shots were fired by both sides. From the river bank, more Indian riflemen emerged. Fort rifles cracked and echoed, and there was a hail of bullets. Daniel shook off a warrior and knocked Blackfish flat on his back in a furious dash back to the fort. A tomahawk flew overhead; Daniel ducked and was grazed on the back of the head and between the shoulder blades. His brother was wounded by a bullet but stood up again and kept running. Amazingly, Daniel and all his men survived a barrage of an estimated two hundred rounds of fire. The fort gate slammed shut. The battle for Boonesborough had begun.

In the first volley, a sleepy lookout lounging in a blockhouse tumbled to the ground. He landed unhurt, but reportedly had fourteen bullets through his clothing.

Daniel moved among the people as quickly as he could, giving orders and encouragement. After ten minutes of intense gunfire, there was an eerie quiet. The Indians had fallen back with their dead and wounded. Boonesborough had its own wounded to attend to. Daniel's injury was dressed. Then he removed the bullet from Squire's shoulder. His brother went to bed with an ax for the "last action," when it came.

During the dark, windy night that followed, the Indians set fire to a pile of flax just outside the fort wall. Daniel ordered a tunnel dug under it and a trench constructed. Two men crawled out with buckets to extinguish the flames and returned safely. A slave was not so lucky. While guarding the open trench, he was shot and killed.

The next morning, the Indians rode away, making a lot of noise. But Daniel was not taken in by this trick. The Indians were not retreating, only attempting to lure foolish settlers outside the fort. Daniel made sure the gate stayed shut. Before long, the Indians were back.

Gunfire blazed for a full day. Then the Boonesborough defenders heard a strange noise. It wasn't artillery; it was the sound of axes biting into trees. What was happening out there? Looking over the palisade, the settlers could see the Indians driving logs into the ground. There were other disturbing signs. Upstream, the Kentucky River appeared clear; downstream, the current was muddy. What did it all mean?

A tunnel. Under the guidance of de Quindre, the Indians were using fancy siege techniques. They were digging a tunnel from the river to the fort. The attackers meant to shovel under a Boonesborough wall and let it collapse. If that didn't work, a powder charge would be exploded where it would do the most damage. As soon as the palisade fell, warriors would surge inside the fort. Boonesborough would be finished.

A crude watchtower went up so that the enemy's work could be seen more clearly. Day and night the anxious settlers heard reports. Dirt was being dumped into the river. The tunnel was getting longer.

The solution was for the settlers to start immediately digging their own tunnel, a kind of countermine. Daniel ordered a four-foot-deep passage that would run under the cabins, parallel to the fort's river wall; at some point, it would cross the Indian tunnel. If the settlers were lucky, maybe they'd be able to collapse the invaders' tunnel. If not, maybe they'd be able to pick off attackers as they came through.

Digging a tunnel was hot, exhausting work in the blazing September sun. The Boonesborough countermine was no secret. Earth was dumped over the palisades in plain view as a kind of warning.

Settlers' tempers flared as water, food, and ammunition became scarce. The muggy heat was stifling. Thirsty cattle inside the fort lowed pathetically. Children cried. There was little sleep and no escape from anxiety. All the settlers knew there was only a feeble wooden palisade between them and death. Would it hold?

Sniping by both sides continued. Sometimes the Indians found their mark. Jemima was hit in the backside; she was more humiliated than injured. A settler standing guard was not so lucky. When a bullet bounced against a rock blocking a fort loophole, the fractured rock pieces flew into his forehead. He died before morning.

Daniel was a favorite sniper target. One day, he was hit as he crossed the common. Fortunately, the wound was not serious. But the Indians thought they had killed him and chanted loudly, "We killed your Boone! Old Boone dead now!"

As soon as he was bandaged, Daniel took special pleasure in shouting back, "Hey, here's old Boone, back from the grave!"

The digging and the taunts never stopped.

"What you doing down there?" a Boonesborough rifleman yelled from his lookout to the Indians below.

"Digging a hole. Blow you all to hell tonight. Maybe so? And what are you doing?"

"Digging to meet you [with] a hole large enough to bury five hundred of you sons of bitches."

On the sixth day of the siege, a cool gray mist rolled in from the northwest. That night the Indians made another all-out attack. Blazing arrows were shot onto cabin roofs. The Indians swept the area with bullets to keep anyone from quenching the flames with what little water was left. In spite of the danger, some of the settlers dashed out to pull burning shingles off and fling them safely beyond the palisades.

It seemed hopeless. Simon Kenton and Alexander Montgomery, who had been on a scouting mission when the attack began, watched helplessly from the surrounding hills. Another observer hidden in the woods was Boonesborough resident William Patton. Patton witnessed the fiery attack on the night of September 16. He later said he heard Boonesborough women and children screaming. Certain that this was the end and unable to stomach the sights and sounds any longer, he slipped away to Logan's Station with the news that Boonesborough had fallen.

Inside the fort, smoke rose and flames licked log walls. All that stood between the settlers and massacre was slowly being burned away. Some men suggested escape. Daniel quickly put an end to that idea. Every man had to stay to defend the women and children.

Just as Boonesborough settlers expected the sound of war whoops, they heard the hiss of rain. The fires sputtered out. But there was no wild cheering. Everyone knew this was only a lull in the action.

All night it rained, and the barrels and catch basins danced with water. The next day, the dismal grayness made the people gloomier—especially when they could hear the Indians digging only ten feet away.

There were more quarrels. Colonel Callaway stomped about, spreading rumors of "Boone's betrayal to the Indians" and asserting that he, Callaway, was more fit to lead. But the people didn't listen. Most felt that Daniel knew best what the Indians would do next. They trusted him as they trusted no one else. It was up to him to pull them through.

Daniel did not have any answers to their dilemma. After a week without sound sleep or decent food and burdened by responsibility for every life in Boonesborough, he was weary beyond words. As the scrape-scrape-scrape of enemy shovels came closer, he may have wondered if he should have left Boonesborough when he had the chance and gone off to North Carolina after Rebecca.

In the afternoon, the sky grew blacker. It rained hard all through the night. The shivering settlers waited. At any moment, they expected the Indians' tunnel to reach the fort walls. The end would come soon.

On September 18, an hour before a cloudless dawn, the sentinels sensed something strange. It wasn't just that the rain had stopped. It was something else—sudden, deafening silence. Everyone listened. They could not hear the digging. A sentry shouted that the Indians' tunnel had collapsed! He could see caved-in sections filled with rainwater.

And what was even more incredible, the Indians had left.

After seven days of digging, the disgusted warriors had given up. The rain put out their fire arrows and, in the end, collapsed their tunnel. They decided the spirits were against their work. De Quindre had shouted and cursed at them, but with no success. The Indians rode empty-handed back to Chillicothe to plan another attack.

In disbelief, the settlers wandered out through the open Boonesborough gates. Was it really over? Were they actually still alive? Some were stunned into dumb silence. Others were silly with laughter.

The Indians had lost an estimated thirty-seven men. The settlers had buried two, and four others were wounded. Crops were trampled or burned; most of the cattle had been destroyed. It had been the longest siege ever in Kentucky. Nearly 125 pounds of lead had been shot at the settlers. This was later picked out of cabin walls and the palisade and melted in molds to make new bullets.

Probably no one in Boonesborough realized the consequence of their survival. As Daniel stood gazing about the wreckage, Gen. George Rogers Clark's troops were marching to capture British-held forts at Cahokia, Kaskaskia, and Vincennes in present-day Illinois and Indiana. Clark would continue the thrust, successfully attacking Fort Detroit and taking Hamilton prisoner. If Boonesborough had fallen into British hands, all Kentucky settlements would have, too. Clark's supply lines and only exit would have been cut, ending his campaign to secure American control from the Appalachian Mountains to the Mississippi.

Boonesborough was the grim test. Its survival meant that Kentucky and the Ohio River valley wilderness would remain secure as part of the fledgling nation that called itself America.

Chapter Sixteen

Guilty of Treason?

The triumphant news about Boonesborough traveled quickly, all the way to the East Coast, where the Revolution had reached a turning point. After the British had been defeated by the Continental Army at Saratoga, New York, in October 1777, the French government decided to openly recognize the United States and support its struggle with supplies and soldiers. In July 1778, the first fleet of French warships reached America. Now it seemed as if the Continental Army might have a chance to win.

For three years, Britain had failed to put down the American rebellion—at a cost of nearly ten thousand British soldiers' lives. Now she faced the firepower of her old enemy, France. It was time to change strategy, the British decided. Instead of targeting the North, the new focus of attack would be the South, where the British hoped to find more Loyalist support.

Choosing sides—for England or for a new, independent government—was no easy matter for colonists during the Revolutionary War. While many felt strongly that America should be free and independent, others, called Loyalists or Tories, were content and even proud to be loyal to England. The war caused neighbor to fight neighbor, brother to fight brother.

For many people in the West, the survival of the land they had worked so hard to settle was more important than political ideas. As long as Britain threatened the settlements by supporting Indian raiders, Daniel and most Kentuckians threw their support to the Americans.

But the strain of uncertain and often conflicting loyalties was beginning to cause problems in Boonesborough. Rumors surfaced that Daniel might be a British sympathizer, or worse yet, a British spy. People wondered what went on when Boone met with the Hair Buyer, Hamilton, in Detroit. And why was his wife living with British-sympathizing Tory relatives back in North Carolina?

Fanning the flames of this gossip was Colonel Callaway. He still smarted from the humiliation he had felt at being stepped over as Boonesborough commander. What he wanted, quite simply, was Daniel's arrest and court-martial on the charge of treason. It was Boone, Colonel Callaway said, who was responsible for the siege. It was Boone who had made that dirty deal with the Indians. (Colonel Callaway ignored the fact that he, too, had signed Blackfish's treaty.)

Colonel Callaway's charges were only as amazing as people's desire to believe them. Now that the danger was gone, there were those who rather liked the idea of the famous Daniel Boone getting his comeuppance. They had heard stories of how Blackfish had treated him in a princely fashion. What made Daniel think he was so special?

"Boone never deserved anything of the country," sniffed Keziah French, Colonel Callaway's sister. Her words cut to the quick.

Lies and exaggerations snowballed, but not one Boonesborough officer would press charges. Colonel Callaway had to ask the leader of another station to mount the court-martial. In early October, Daniel was placed under arrest and taken away from Boonesborough to the Logan's Station blockhouse. He would be court-martialed that month. The news of his arrest spread like wildfire through the settlements.

Graying and haggard, the back of his neck scarred from the tomahawk wound he had received during the siege, Daniel was filled with sadness and bitter disappointment. He had just risked his life for the very people who were now publicly humiliating him. He wrote a letter to Rebecca so full of uncharacteristic swearing that his shocked wife cut it to shreds.

Daniel was accused of favoring the British government and was charged with the treasonable act of seeking Fort Boonesborough's surrender to the British and their Indian allies. He was also charged with purposefully surrendering the salt makers to the enemy. As a prisoner of the Shawnee, he was said to have "engaged with Governor Hamilton" to remove the Boonesborough settlers to Detroit. It was said that at the end of August he had dangerously weakened the fort by encouraging a party of men to go with him to raid Shawnee villages. Finally, Boone had taken officers to the Indian camp "on the pretense of making peace" when Blackfish was about to attack Boonesborough.

Free-for-all court-martials weren't unusual in Kentucky, with its unruly militia. The courtroom erupted into arguments and accusations. People pointed fingers at Daniel. They pointed fingers at each other. Daniel had no witnesses to come to his defense. The outcome of the trial looked grim. If Daniel were found guilty of treason, he would be stripped of all military commissions and would lose his good name. Because the country was at war, he might even face execution as a traitor.

At last, Daniel was asked to say a few words in his own defense. Quietly, he explained what he had done and why he had done it. While in the enemy's power, he had used tricks and lies in an attempt to help his own people. When he escaped and came back to Boonesborough, he did not turn around and flee to his family in North Carolina. Instead, he stayed with the rest to be "tomahawked and shot, to share their perils and sleepless nights, and to risk his very life to save them. He thought that sufficient evidence of his devotion to the American cause."[1]

[1] All the official papers describing the court-martial have disappeared — perhaps destroyed by a relative or friend intent on protecting Daniel's good name. Only one observer, Daniel Trabue, kept a reliable account of the trial in his diary, from which this quote is taken.

When asked if he were a British sympathizer, Daniel reminded the judge that seven other men, including Callaway, had signed a British oath of allegiance because they also believed it a bloodless way to meet Blackfish's terms. He neither shared nor condemned Rebecca's relatives' political beliefs. He had only done what *he* felt was right as an American soldier. He was not guilty.

The audience listened. All the members of the court found Daniel innocent. In fact, much to Colonel Callaway's displeasure, Daniel was promoted to the rank of major for "his brave actions in saving the settlements from destruction."

With the court-martial behind him, Daniel set out for North Carolina to convince his wife and children to return with him. Rebecca refused his request for a full year; she had seen enough hardship and heartbreak in the wilds of Kentucky. While Daniel tried to persuade her, troubles between Kentucky settlers and Indians continued.

In the spring of 1779, two hundred militiamen made a bloody surprise attack at the Shawnee camp near Little Chillicothe after the Shawnee had fired at passing flatboats on the Ohio. Blackfish was one of the Indians wounded. One account says the Shawnee chief somehow thought Sheltowee was among the white attackers and tried to surrender, thinking that his adopted son would save his life. Wouldn't the white man's medicine cure his wounds? But there was no surrender; the militia destroyed Indian homes and crops and withdrew. A few weeks passed and Blackfish died of infection. Daniel was deeply saddened when he heard the story.

That fall, Daniel packed all the family's belongings, loaded the children into a wagon, and organized a sizable caravan of relatives and friends.[2] Only then did Rebecca finally agree to make the trip. As Daniel's caravan rolled into Boonesborough in October 1779, he saw a booming

[2] Among those who returned with Daniel was a boyhood friend from Pennsylvania, Abraham Lincoln, the grandfather of the man who would one day become president. Daniel was also accompanied by his brother Ned and Ned's family.

128

town overflowing with immigrants—in spite of Indian raids. Gen. George Rogers Clark's success in the Northwest capturing British posts had been enough to convince settlers to pour over the mountains again. Boonesborough had just harvested its largest corn crop. A school had been started, and plans had been made to build a ferry across the Kentucky River.

There were many unfamiliar faces. While he was gone, some of Daniel's oldest and best friends had died or had moved on to less crowded areas. Game was scarce, so Daniel loaded his packhorses and took his family five miles northwest to a small stream where he had a land claim called Boone's Station. It was there that Daniel, Rebecca, and their sons ten-year-old Daniel Morgan and six-year-old Jesse spent what was called "the Hard Winter." That year the rivers froze solid and snow covered the ground from November until the end of January.

During the spring of 1780, Daniel went east to file more land claims. Several eager friends and neighbors gave him money to do the same for them. He left with nearly $50,000 in cash in his saddlebags.

Unfortunately, every last penny was stolen at a Virginia inn. Daniel returned to Kentucky empty-handed, feeling worse because much of the lost money had belonged to his friends. During the years that followed, he struggled to pay everything back.

The Indian attacks were frequent in early 1780. During a five-day period in March, there were nine raids near Daniel's home. Three settlers were killed, and two were taken prisoner. One of those brutally murdered was Colonel Callaway. His mutilated body was found near the Kentucky River, where he had been building his new ferry business. He was lying face-down in the mud, scalped.

Not long after, while out scouting in the woods, Daniel himself barely escaped with his life when confronted by two braves who tried to follow him into a canebrake. With only time to make one shot, he waited until the two braves were lined up in his rifle sights. His bullet killed the first and injured the second.

By May 1780, the British had taken the entire southern Continental Army at Savannah and at Charleston, where nearly 5,500 patriots surrendered. A second army raised by the Continental Congress was rushed to Camden, South Carolina, in August 1780, where it too, suffered complete defeat. American morale was at a low ebb. The British decided to take advantage of the situation by increasing the supply of arms to their Indian allies in the West. Major de Peyster, who took over Hamilton's command in Detroit, ordered 188 tomahawks, 475 dozen "Scalping knives good blades & solid handles," not to mention 750 pounds of vermilion war paint (the Indians' favorite color) and 8,000 pounds of good gunpowder.

During early summer, seven hundred Shawnee and Great Lakes Indians commanded by British Capt. Henry Bird marched into Kentucky to make quick work of the Kentucky forts. Bird had two cannons and bombardiers to man them. In June, his army attacked Ruddle's Station with field guns, and rather than be blown to bits, the fort surrendered. It was the first in Kentucky to give in to the British. A week later, nearby Martin's Station fell. Two other abandoned forts were burned.

The Indians were excited by victory. Captain Bird uneasily sensed they weren't listening to him anymore. He had been warned earlier about "the Fickleness of the Indians and their aversion to controul." With considerable difficulty, he attempted to transport several hundred Kentucky captives, many of them women and children, back to Canada. Reports said the trail was scattered with tomahawked bodies of those too weak to keep up. The site of abandoned Ruddle's Station was later described being littered with "little wheels, plough irons, blacksmith's tools, feather beds ripped open, etc., scattered about."

There was no talk of peace, only more war. In retaliation, Daniel and white settlers burned Chillicothe and other Indian settlements. The British continued to goad the Indians to retake western lands. Every household felt the loss of a friend or family member.

In the fall of 1780, Daniel and his brother Ned, who looked very much like him, were collecting salt at Upper Blue Licks near the Licking River. As they started home along a creek, they saw a bear. Daniel wounded the animal and pursued it downstream. Ned stayed behind, resting on the shore, cracking hickory nuts and keeping an eye on the horses. Suddenly, Daniel heard the crack of a rifle and, one account says, an Indian shouting, "It's Boone! We killed old Boone!"

As fast as he could, Daniel darted into a canebrake. He could hear the Indians' dog close on his trail. It was one thing to hide from a person and quite another to hide from a sniffing dog. Daniel had dropped his ramrod and could not reload his gun. Quickly, he slashed a piece of cane and used it to jam powder and shot into the barrel. He crouched, waiting for the dog to appear. He shot it and made his escape.

When he sorrowfully returned the next day to get his brother's body, he discovered that the Indians had taken their salt, horses, and, worst of all, they had cut off Ned's head. Daniel was certain the Indians thought they had killed *him*. He tracked the attackers to the Ohio but never found them. Still grieving, on the way back he hunted a year's supply of meat for his brother's widow and their six children.

The year after his brother's death, Daniel was promoted to the rank of lieutenant colonel in the militia and appointed sheriff and surveyor of Fayette County. In all of Kentucky, which was still considered part of Virginia, there were now nearly twenty-five thousand people. Daniel's first political job came when he was sent to Richmond to represent his neighbors at the Virginia Assembly, which was presided over by Thomas Jefferson.

When the British troops came uncomfortably close, the assembly was forced to flee to Charlottesville, Virginia. In June 1781, the British attacked Charlottesville, nearly capturing Jefferson as he rode out of town. Daniel was one of the handful who stayed behind to help load county records into a wagon.

Dressed in plain buckskin and moccasins, he looked like anything but a legislator. Nevertheless, the British stopped him as he was riding slowly out of town. Daniel told the officers he was a farmer on his way home. The soldiers probably would have believed him, but just then one of Daniel's friends called out, "Wait a minute, Colonel! I'll go with you."

"Colonel, is it?" said a British officer, glad to capture someone important.

Daniel was locked up in a dusty coal house, where he spent the night singing songs. The next day, he was called to explain exactly what kind of colonel he was. His face still smeared with coal grime, Daniel smiled. The whole thing was a joke, he explained. "Colonel" was just a name people called him. The British officer believed every word and sent the crude-looking farmer on his way.

Daniel hurried forty miles west in time to make the next Virginia Assembly session. Sometime during the summer, Daniel returned to Boone's Station. On March 2, 1781, forty-one-year-old Rebecca had delivered their tenth child, a boy named Nathan. One story goes that when Daniel arrived home, his wife lined up their new son and two grandchildren, born about the same time. She challenged him to guess which one was his. He did.

Chapter Seventeen

Death at Blue Licks

In the first nine months of 1781, 131 people in Jefferson County, Kentucky—nearly thirteen percent of that county's total population—were killed or taken prisoner by the Indians. Without any kind of standing army, Kentucky settlers depended on their own militia volunteers for protection—the same men who were trying to feed families and plant and harvest crops. The last years of the Revolutionary War spread the settlers' defenses even thinner. Many Kentucky forts and stations lost their best riflemen when they were sent north to fight with George Rogers Clark.

Unfortunately, Clark did not always make the best use of Kentucky manpower. Daniel was frustrated when Clark ordered him to lead one hundred men to build a fort at the Licking River. As soon as Daniel and his men arrived, Clark changed his mind. Daniel was told to take the men to Louisville and build a "row galley," an armed boat with oars that was supposed to keep the Indians from crossing the Ohio. While time was wasted building a floating fortress that Indians could easily avoid, "our own frontiers [are left] open and unguarded," Daniel later complained in a letter to the governor of Virginia.

Even though a large British force surrendered at Yorktown, Virginia, in October, 1781, fighting in some areas continued for two more years.

In Kentucky, there were more attacks than ever. The British viewed Kentucky as their last toehold in North America. They worked the Indians into a frenzy.

The year 1782 came to be known as "the Year of Blood." In March, a group of Wyandot raiders killed a young girl and captured a man fifteen miles from Boonesborough. When a group of twenty-five settlers retaliated, all but six were killed. In June, a Delaware war party on the Sandusky River in present-day Ohio drove nearly five hundred soldiers into retreat, captured their leader, and burned him alive. When Nathaniel Hart, an old friend of Daniel's, was murdered within a mile of Boonesborough, a party of sixty settlers rode off in pursuit of the attackers and was immediately ambushed.

In early August, a group of three hundred Wyandots and fifty white soldiers led by British Capt. William Caldwell slipped undiscovered across the Ohio River. They headed for Bryan's Station, only a few miles from Boonesborough. This large fort, built by Rebecca's relatives and others from North Carolina, had nearly forty cabins and palisades twelve feet high. It was guarded by forty-four riflemen.

One story says that at the last moment a swift rider alerted Bryan's Station of an attack. But even as the settlers quickly prepared for the worst, they knew the British and Indians had already secretly surrounded them. For the people in Bryan's Station to survive, they'd need water. The daily supply had not yet been collected. But how could anyone leave the fort when the Indians waited in ambush?

The settlers decided the women would go for water at the little creek down the hill, the same way they did every morning. The Indians would then be convinced that no one in the fort was aware of their presence.

Which women were brave or foolhardy enough to make the long trip to the creek? To avoid any hint of favoritism, it was decided that every last one of the thirty-five mothers and daughters at Bryan's Station would go. It's hard to imagine everyone went willingly. The women and girls knelt in prayer, then they slipped off their moccasins and left them in a row, knowing they could run faster barefoot. When the gate was opened, they all went out, swinging buckets and gourds, "stringing along, two or three together, as naturally as possible," one water gatherer later wrote. "A paler-faced crowd of women was never seen."

Sure enough, they were surrounded by Indians. A pair of moccasins and the flash of a tomahawk were spied in the underbrush. The girls and women must have felt the presence of eyes everywhere—staring, studying their every movement. They tried not to look around as they chatted, dipped buckets into the water, and walked back to the fort. They did not hurry, even though they wanted to run to safety as fast as their bare feet could take them.

The Indians let the water carriers go. Maybe they supposed the women would soon be useful prisoners.

The women and girls made it back inside the fort, and the gate slammed shut. By midday, the Indians gave up waiting and began the attack. Two Kentuckians were killed. The Indians tried to set the fort on fire but were unsuccessful. That afternoon, summoned by a messenger, a troop of militiamen from Lexington finally arrived. The next morning the angry British and Indians galloped away, having burned all the crops and slaughtered six hundred cattle, hogs, and sheep.

Daniel and a relief party arrived just in time to witness the smoldering destruction. Should they pursue the attackers or wait for the five hundred men they knew were coming from other settlements?

Revenge was on most of the men's minds. Not wishing to appear a coward, Lt. Col. John Todd, the commanding officer, agreed they had plenty of men to deal with the raiders.

One hundred eighty-two men rode hard on the Indians' trail. Daniel was in charge of all the men from his county. Included were many of his wife's relatives, his son-in-law, his nephew, and his twenty-three-year-old son, Israel, who almost stayed home because he had been ill.

Daniel wondered aloud why the Indians were making it so easy to follow them. Were the soldiers falling into an obvious ambush?

After riding nearly thirty miles, the militia made camp a few miles below the Licking River. Most of the officers were certain they'd victoriously overtake the raiders the next day. Daniel was not so sure.

In the morning, the militia followed the river to the hills overlooking Blue Licks, a salt spring located on the Licking River. Below, on the opposite shore, they saw a handful of Indians dart into the trees.

The men were anxious for a fight. Daniel cautioned Lieutenant Colonel Todd not to ride into the ambush waiting on the other side of the river. It was likely they were badly outnumbered; why not wait for reinforcements? There was no reason to fight the Indians on their terms.

Todd shook his head. He worried what people might think of him if he let someone else tell him what to do. Wasn't he supposed to be in charge?

Daniel pleaded for patience. Todd reluctantly sent a small group of scouts across the river to explore the ridge. They came back without seeing anything, just as Daniel had known they would. The Indians had no intention of revealing themselves.

"We do not have time to wait for old ladies!" a hot-headed militiaman named Hugh McGary shouted. The others cheered in agreement.

Daniel again urged Todd not to lead the men into a trap.

The commanding officer nervously observed the restlessness of his men. Would they do as he told them? In such a thrown-together, frontier army, soldiers didn't stand for much in the way of protocol or formal orders. They considered themselves equal to their leaders, and they often did exactly as they pleased.

"All who are not damned cowards, follow me and I'll soon show you where the Indians are!" McGary taunted. He whipped his horse down to the river with the others close behind. No one could stop them, not even Daniel. He followed with his own men. The current churned with splashing, galloping horses.

At that moment, Daniel may have remembered another river crossing, another hot summer day, another group of exultant soldiers certain of easy victory. It was twenty-seven years earlier that he had witnessed General Braddock's defeat. History was about to repeat itself tragically.

On the other side of the river, the Kentuckians dismounted and walked. In the lead was an advance guard of twenty-five soldiers. They walked along a buffalo trace that led up a hill. On the other side was a ravine thick with undergrowth. There was an eerie silence.

When the last soldier crossed the hill's ridge, two hundred hidden rifles blazed away at a range of only forty yards. In less than five minutes, all but three of the twenty-five advance guard were mowed down.

The rest of the militia rushed forward and attempted to take positions behind trees in the ravine. There was so little room to maneuver between the fallen bodies and the undergrowth that many were caught in the cross fire. Lieutenant Colonel Todd was shot. Even though Daniel and his men managed to force the Indians back about a hundred yards, most of the militia was driven toward the river, which was nearly a mile away. When Daniel realized that the situation was nearly hopeless, he ordered his men, too, to run for their lives to the Licking.

Few made it. The Indians followed swiftly, tomahawks flashing.

Desperately, Daniel now tried to lead the rest of his men west through the woods. He knew this terrain like the back of his hand—if he could only get them to the ford near Indian Creek, they might be safe! Israel crouched behind a tree, covering the retreat. From somewhere a horse appeared. Daniel grabbed the bridle and urged his son to mount and escape.

"Give it to someone else, Father," Israel replied, "and we will go together."

Daniel let the horse go. In that instant he heard a rifle crack and saw his son crumple to the ground, a bullet lodged in his chest. Blood filled Israel's mouth. Daniel took him in his arms and carried him down a hill through the woods. He spun around; a Wyandot stood less than four feet away. Holding the boy's body in his left arm, Daniel fired with his right and shot the man point-blank.

At the ford, Daniel struggled to keep Israel's head above water. He stumbled out of the stream and kept running. One account says that Daniel remembered a nearby cave where he thought they'd be safe. He took the boy there and laid him tenderly on the ground. But it was too late.

After a long time, Daniel finally stood up and started back to Boone's Station to tell Rebecca that their second oldest son was dead.

The Battle of Blue Licks was the last major confrontation between the Americans and the British and their Indian allies during the Revolutionary War. Israel Boone was among seventy-seven fatalities. Twelve men were injured. Daniel buried his son at Boone's Station. Those whose mutilated bodies were found along the river were buried in a common grave.

Daniel did not lay blame on any of the officers who led the charge on Blue Licks. He simply stated the facts in a letter to the governor of Virginia. He also described the serious dangers faced by the Kentucky settlers. Less than 130 militiamen could be counted on in all of Fayette County. "I have encouraged the people here in this County all that I could, but I can no longer Encourage my neighbors, nor myself, to risque our lives here at such Extraordinary hazzards. The Inhabitants of these Counties are very much alarmed at the thoughts of the Indians bringing another Campaign into our Country this fall, which if it should be the case, will Break these settlements. . . But are we to be totally forgotten. I hope not."

After Blue Licks, even those who had steadfastly remained during the hard years in Kentucky began to flee. One man offered another "the whole of 1,400 acres of his pre-emption. . . for one little black horse to carry his family back to Virginia."

Daniel first learned that the Americans had signed a treaty with the British on April 19, 1783, when a breathless rider appeared at Boonesborough's gates with "PEACE" written on a paper stuck in his cap. The war was finally over.

But the Indian attacks would go on, even though the English were no longer directly supplying war paint and scalping knives. Old wounds did not heal quickly. For the next eleven years, until Gen. Anthony Wayne's brutal victory over the Shawnee at Fallen Timbers in 1794, there would be little peace in Kentucky. Broken promises and atrocities on both sides continued. There seemed no workable, peaceful solution. Kentucky would remain, as Daniel said, "full of freshly widowed and orphaned."

Daniel, Rebecca, and several of their children lived at Boone's Station until 1783 when the sheriff rode up and announced they had to move. The land, he said, belonged to someone else. Rebecca packed their belongings. It was difficult to leave the place they'd worked so hard to build, the place where one son and Daniel's brother Ned were buried.

Daniel later told about a close encounter with Indians that occurred around this time. While hanging his tobacco to cure from the ceiling of a shed near his home, he was startled by four braves who were aiming their rifles at him. He stood helpless, without a gun or weapon.

"Well Boone, we got you good this time. You no get away any more. We carry you off to Chillicothe."

As he had so many times in the past, Daniel acted delighted to see his Shawnee brothers. He recognized a few from his captivity nearly five years before. "Well, old friends! I'm so glad to see you," he replied, never once pausing from his work.

"Come down, Boone, now!" they demanded impatiently, wary of his tricks.

Daniel didn't stop talking. He chatted on about tobacco curing, all the time gathering an armful of tobacco leaves. Suddenly, he swept the whole mess into their upturned faces. Choking and blinded by the leaves and dust, the Indians were pushed aside by Daniel as he leapt from the loft and raced into his house. Sheltowee had fooled them again. Daniel locked the door and had a good laugh.

Chapter Eighteen

Missouri: a New Dream

For ten years, beginning in 1779, Daniel steadily entered claims in Kentucky for more than ten thousand acres, much of which were grants for military service or payment for surveys. His neighbors and brother, Squire, made equally lavish claims. To own land meant independence and security. Daniel was typical of most Kentuckians. He was absolutely spellbound by "the rapturous idea of property."

By 1786, Daniel's property was said to amount to nearly a hundred thousand acres. But mismanagement, legal problems, and conflicting claims chipped away at his holdings. In Kentucky's early settlement rush, surveys were often haphazard. Nobody was sure where one claim started and ended. As time went on, boundaries overlapped like shingles on a roof. Property maps showed so many "shingled" claim lines that the maps resembled crazy quilts. The situation became more perplexing when property changed hands. When settlers went to court over boundary conflicts, it was not unusual for them to lose land they had cleared, plowed, planted, and defended with their lives.

✗Few, however, lost as much land as Daniel Boone. "Unacquainted with the niceties of the law, the lands I was enabled to locate, through my own ignorance, were swallowed up by better claims," said Daniel.

It didn't help that Kentucky attracted sophisticated speculators who were eager to make quick profits at the expense of others. In one phony land deal, a slick Easterner cheated Daniel out of nearly ten thousand acres. Some say it was this same charming swindler who later told the story of Daniel's life to a schoolteacher by the name of John Filson, a man who spent a year with Daniel, scribbling down his reminiscences.

The "autobiography" Filson wrote entitled *The Adventures of Col. Daniel Boon*, was published in 1784 as an appendix to Filson's *The Discovery, Settlement and Present State of Kentucke*. The epic qualities of Daniel's story made the book a big success in Europe, where it was printed in English, French, and German. A new edition rolled off the presses in Philadelphia in 1787, renamed *Adventures of Colonel Daniel Boone, One of the Original Settlers of Kentucke*.[1] When asked if the book were true, Daniel was said to have replied sarcastically, "Not a lie in it."

Among the literary elite in the salons of Europe, "the noble savage" was all the rage. Daniel Boone seemed to be the living example of a "natural man" unfettered by the shackles of society—the very type idealized by French philosopher Jean Jacques Rousseau (1712-1778) and his followers. Before many Americans outside Kentucky even heard of Daniel Boone, there were Europeans writing poems, novels, and plays about him. Daniel Boone would one day become an international celebrity, inspiring Lord Byron (1788-1824) to write in *Don Juan*:

[1] Following in Filson's footsteps, Timothy Flint (1780-1840) popularized his favorite American frontier hero in a series of biographies. Between 1833 and 1868, more than fourteen different editions of Flint's *The First Man of the West: The Life and Exploits of Col. Daniel Boone* were printed. Daniel Bryan (1795-1866), one of Rebecca's relatives, eulogized Boone in a long epic poem published in 1813, entitled *The Mountain Muse, Comprising the Adventures of Daniel Boone and The Power of Virtuous and Refined Beauty*.

James Fenimore Cooper (1789-1851) immortalized the Boone legend further. He based his heroes in five novels in the *Leatherstocking Tales*, written between 1823-1841, on Daniel's "biography". Cooper's *The Last of the Mohicans* includes the rescue of Daniel's kidnapped daughter and friends from the Indians. American painters who used Daniel Boone in their portraits and landscapes included: Horatio Greenough, Chester Harding, John James Audubon, Thomas Sully, and George C. Bingham. Bingham's "The Emigration of Daniel Boone," painted in 1851, shows Daniel leading a group of settlers into the West, the promised land.

Of the great names which in our faces stare
Is Daniel Boone, backwoodsman of Kentucky.

In the meantime, Daniel received no money from Filson's popular publication and was struggling to earn a living and get out of debt. In 1783, he and his family moved to Limestone to try running a tavern. Rebecca did the cooking. He tried his hand at surveying. He even tried digging the medicinal root, ginseng, to sell in Philadelphia. But on the way to market the boat overturned on the Ohio, and the soggy cargo was only worth half of what he had hoped. Another time, he tried riding Kentucky horses east to sell. But when they arrived, they were too scrawny to be worth anything.

To see if he could change his luck, Daniel moved his family some time in 1789 or 1790 to Campbell's Creek in Kanawha County. Whenever he could, he went hunting and trapping with his son Nathan. Although he was tangled in lawsuits, Daniel still had his Kanawha County neighbors' respect. They petitioned that he be appointed commander of the local militia. In 1791, he was elected again to the Virginia Assembly and walked all the way to the state capital in Richmond. But he soon tired of politics and came home. In 1795, the Boones were on the move again. They left the big double log cabin Daniel had built along Campbell's Creek and went to Brushy Fork, near Blue Licks.

Times were changing. Daniel no longer played a central role in the affairs of Kentucky. There were nearly seventy-five thousand Kentuckians living in towns and on farms—not in forts. They considered Daniel part of the region's romantic past. In 1792, Kentucky, which had been settled only twenty years before by Daniel and other pioneers, entered the union as the fifteenth state.

Short of cash again in 1796, Daniel was inspired to write to Kentucky's new governor when he read in the *Kentucky Gazette* that the Wilderness Road was to be widened. "I think myself entitled to the offer of the business," Daniel wrote, "as I first marked out that road in March, 1775, and never received anything for my trouble and suppose I am no

Statesman but I am a woodsman and think myself as capable of marking and cutting that Road as any other man."

But the governor never even answered his letter.

Throughout 1798, Daniel was often asked to act as a witness in lawsuits involving conflicting land claims. He had worked as a surveyor, and he knew the land and its "markings" better than anyone else. But occasionally, when these lawsuits were lost, Daniel received threats— sometimes against his life. He was said to have told one relative, "In time of peace my own Kentucky has become more dangerous to me than it had been in Indian times." Exhausted by the "vexation," he decided he did not want to die among such quarreling people.

At sixty-four years of age, Daniel gave his last bit of land to a relative with instructions to divide it among those to whom he owed money. Creditors—some real, some only interested in an easy dollar—swarmed with demands. In no time, all of Daniel's Kentucky land was gone. His "creditors'" greed was the last straw. He would leave Kentucky forever.

For sometime Daniel had been aware of the travels of twenty-five-year-old Daniel Morgan, who was said to have looked more like his father than any of the other Boone children. Three years earlier, in 1795, Daniel Morgan had gone to explore what is now known as Missouri. This land west of the Mississippi was owned by the Spanish government. Daniel Morgan reported to his father that the country, marked simply as "Upper Louisiana" on most maps, was open and full of excellent game. A meeting between Daniel Morgan and Lt. Gov. Don Zenon Trudeau resulted in an interesting offer. The Spanish wanted settlers who would farm the land, discourage the Indians, and keep out the British. They were even willing to bend their law allowing only Catholic homesteaders. They realized where someone like Daniel Boone went, others would follow.

Daniel was offered one thousand arpents, the equivalent of 850 acres,[2] if he would lead a group of settlers into the country. Each family who came with him would receive four hundred arpents. In 1799, the

[2] One arpent equals .85 acres.

same year that George Washington died, sixty-five-year-old Daniel Boone was beginning his life all over. He had made up his mind it was time to move west again. Now he had a new dream: Missouri. He cut down a yellow poplar and began making a sixty-foot canoe to carry his large family and their supplies down the Ohio River to the Mississippi, then north on the Mississippi to the Missouri River.

It was a clear morning in September when the large group left Kentucky. Once again, the clan of Boones and their relations by marriage made the move together. And once again, good land was the lure. A few other friends and neighbors decided to tag along as well. Squire, Daniel Morgan, and Nathan were in charge of the canoes. Women and children rode between the piles of supplies. Daniel and two of his sons-in-law, Flanders Callaway and William Hayes, drove the cattle and horses by land.

There were crowds to see them off. Everyone wanted a glimpse of the famous Daniel Boone. Everyone wanted to know why he was leaving Kentucky. He needed elbow room, Daniel said. It was as simple as that. According to one story, when a neighbor moved in only seventy miles from him, he had told Rebecca, "Old woman, we must move, for now they are crowding us."

Daniel walked every foot of the seven-hundred-mile journey. When he and his family arrived in Missouri, they moved to the farthest western region, the Femme Osage District. Daniel did not build a cabin on his own land; for convenience, he built it on Daniel Morgan's property, overlooking the Missouri. Later, he helped his son Nathan build a handsome blue limestone house on another piece of land not far away. Some say Daniel carved the sunburst designs on the walnut fireplace mantel. Later, Daniel and Rebecca lived there with Nathan and his family.

Hunting in the surrounding wilderness was excellent. Another hundred families were convinced to come west, and Daniel was awarded an additional ten thousand arpents by the delighted Spanish governor.

When he wasn't hunting and trapping, Daniel was acting as syndic.

He was appointed in 1800 to this job that made him sheriff, judge, and jury all in one. He sat under a big elm called the "Judgment Tree" and settled disputes. His miserable years in court were put to good use.

Daniel did not believe in ceremony or formal procedures. All he wanted was the truth. And in a dignified, fair manner, he made his decisions—who would receive which cow, who would be punished for disturbing the peace. He did not believe in prison sentences that prevented a man from providing for his family. It was better to be "whipped and cleared." Depending on the offense, a man would receive a lashing and then be on his way. It was justice people could understand, and there was never a single appeal on record.

In 1803, the vast area called Missouri changed hands again. Spain was forced to cede the land back to France. Crippled by war debts, the French emperor Napoleon then sold more than eight hundred thousand square miles to the United States government. The Louisiana Purchase, which stretched from the Mississippi to the Rocky Mountains, from the Canadian border to the Gulf of Mexico, was a real bargain—only fifteen million dollars for vast lands that doubled America's size.

Unfortunately for Daniel, the American government didn't think much of his Spanish claim. He had ignored the rules and had never built a house or planted a crop on his property. As he tried to explain to the officials, he was a hunter, not a farmer. They took away every acre.

Once again, Daniel was landless.

He knew he would not be hungry or homeless. He could always live with his sons, who had managed to legally maintain their huge holdings by building homes and planting crops. And there was still plenty of game. But Daniel was stunned by the loss of so much land.

That year he may have returned briefly to Kentucky to testify about old land surveys. A tree carved with his name and the date 1803 was discovered near Louisville. With characteristic Quaker simplicity, he returned again in 1810 and 1817 to clear his name of debt before he died.[3] On one of these trips, he visited graying Simon Kenton, the daring Boonesborough scout who was now a brigadier general in the Ohio militia. Like Daniel, Kenton did not have an acre of land left to his name. The two old friends never saw each other again.

"No one will say when I am gone, 'Boone is a dishonest man.' I am perfectly willing to die," Daniel said when he had paid his last debts and come home to Missouri with only four bits, approximately fifty cents, in his pocket. By 1814, a special act of Congress awarded Daniel 850 acres—or one-eleventh of the land he had been given by the Spanish. When a group of Kentuckians heard about it, they brought up twenty-five-year old claims. Again, Daniel had to give up every last acre.

Daniel had paid off his creditors, but he was far from his deathbed. When the War of 1812 broke out between Britain and America, he was among the first in the Femme Osage District to enlist. He was insulted when he was told that seventy-eight was too old for active duty.

That spring, he was dealt another, more serious blow. Seventy-four-year-old Rebecca was boiling maple-sugar sap in the woods when she suddenly became ill. She was taken to Jemima's house nearby where she died March 18, 1813. She was buried in the family plot overlooking the wide Missouri. Daniel grieved her passing greatly.

In spite of his age, he never gave up helping people in need. During the War of 1812, the British again stirred up Indian animosity toward the settlers. In the spring of 1815, when a neighboring family was struck by a party of warriors, the wounded father blew a bugle to call for help. Before the attackers left, they tomahawked his three children. Daniel heard the alarm and came at a gallop. "Quiet and unexcited" was the way another neighbor described Daniel as he bandaged the children, removed a bullet from the father, and helped the mother through the

[3] During his 1810 trip back to Kentucky, he met John James Audubon, an engaging young man who was tramping about the countryside drawing pictures of birds and animals. The two were said to have enjoyed each other's company. Daniel showed this future famous naturalist painter how to stun and kill a squirrel so that it did not look damaged when he later posed it for sketches. Audubon also sketched Daniel and later did portraits from the sketches.

premature labor and delivery of a child. The father, two of the children, and the new baby survived. The mother and one tomahawked child died. Throughout, Daniel's help was just as steady as it had been during the dark days at Boonesborough.

During his old age, Daniel's Quaker-based faith remained unshakable. It was a self-styled, contemplative religion he rarely talked about and never flaunted. In his leisure, he sometimes read the Bible or attended various local religious services. However, not one zealous parson—not even his minister brother, Squire—had ever managed to get him to formally join a church. A particularly frustrated churchman once demanded, "Don't you love God?"

"I have always loved God, ever since I can recollect," Daniel was said to have replied quietly.

In a revealing letter to Sarah Day Boone, the sister-in-law who years earlier had taught him how to read, Daniel wrote: "Relating to our family and how we Live in this World and what Chance we Shall have in the next we know Not for my part I am as ignurant as a child. All the Relegan I have to Love and feer god beleve in Jeses Christ Dow all the good to my Nighbour and my Self that I Can and Do as Little Harm as I can help and trust in gods marcy for the Rest."

He had outlived his wife and almost all his friends. Although his own death was something he thought about often, he never stopped being as active as he possibly could, in spite of his rheumatism. He continued his regular hunts and wanderings, even though, before Rebecca died, he used to say it was for his wife that he had trapped beaver and otter to buy her "little delicacies and refreshment"—such as a bit of coffee now and then.

After the War of 1812, Daniel made a series of ambitious wanderings that took him to the plains of Missouri, Kansas, and the Dakotas. On another trip in 1815, with the help of a young slave, the amazing eighty-one-year old journeyed up the Platte River and then by foot traveled all the way to the Rocky Mountains. That winter, he trapped and hunted near the Yellowstone River in present-day Wyoming. His old wandering spirit just never gave up.

As soon as he returned, he announced to Daniel Morgan that the following autumn he would travel even farther. He would visit the "salt mountains, lakes, and ponds about five or six hundred miles west." He was fascinated by what might lie on the western slopes of the Rockies and beyond—all the way to California.

Daniel never had a chance to make the trip. His rheumatism, which had often plagued him in the last years, was becoming increasingly crippling. His eyesight was also beginning to fail. He had to mark his rifle sight with a slip of white paper. During the next six years, he went along on his grandsons' trapping expeditions but always remained close to camp. He helped with the cooking and skinning.

His sense of humor never diminished. One of his last visitors was Chester Harding, an artist from St. Louis. In June 1819, he painted the first—and last—portrait of Daniel from life. One day as he sketched, Harding asked Daniel if he had ever become lost during one of his long hunts, especially since he never used a compass. "No," Daniel was said to have quickly replied, "but I was *bewildered* once for three days."

The finished portrait probably delighted Daniel's huge number of grandchildren—there were nearly fifty in Missouri alone. Daniel said privately that he thought his cheeks looked too sunken, his lips too tightly held over toothless gums.

Harding did manage to capture the brilliant blue of Daniel's eyes, which were as piercing and lively as ever.

The St. Louis artist had experienced a difficult time locating Daniel. Neighbors did not know he was a celebrity. "I found the nearer I got to his dwelling, the less was known of him," Harding wrote.

When he was within two miles of Daniel's house, he stopped to ask a neighbor if he knew a Colonel Boone. The man said he didn't. "Why, yes, you do," said his wife. "It is that white-headed old man who lives on the bottom, near the river."

The white-headed old man she spoke of was frequently seen paddling down the Missouri with a canoe filled with furs. When neighbors passed Jemima's house, they often caught sight of Daniel playing with the young otter and beaver that he had caught and brought home to tame.

His favorite amusement by far, however, was his many grandchildren and great-grandchildren. They enjoyed his exciting stories almost as much as he enjoyed listening to them. "To please [the children], he would partake of the cakes, nuts, and even buttermilk they affectionately presented to him," one relative remembered.

The day he became sick, he rode by carriage from Jemima's to his son Nathan's. Daniel's eighty-sixth birthday was a month away. Two little grandchildren, six-year-old Howard and four-year-old John, made the trip with him, talking and joking all the way. By the time he reached the house, Daniel was in cheerful spirits. He even promised the two boys that he'd soon be well enough to go out with them and gather the hazelnuts they had spotted from the carriage.

After eating a generous portion of his favorite sweet potatoes, Daniel announced he'd like to take a nap. Jemima was one of the last people he spoke with before he retired to his sunny corner room in the big blue limestone house he had helped his son Nathan build. There, on the afternoon of September 26, 1820, surrounded by his family, he quietly died.

Epilogue

Daniel was buried near Rebecca in a cherrywood coffin he had made himself years before. The family graveyard was on a hill overlooking rich Missouri bottomland. The funeral was attended by more friends and relatives than could possibly fit in Nathan's big house, so everyone had to move outside to Jemima and Flanders Callaway's barn.

When legislators in St. Louis, who were working on a constitution for the new state, heard about Daniel's death, they adjourned. They wore black crepe armbands in mourning for twenty days, one for each year Daniel had lived in Missouri.

Myths and legends surrounding his life grew and grew over the years until, for many people, Daniel Boone the man became Daniel Boone the model American Frontier Hero. In the more than two hundred years since his birth, eight counties, twenty towns, and innumerable roads, rivers, parks, and mountains have been named after him—not to mention stores, hotels, toys, movies, and television programs.

In 1845, a rather nasty fight between proud Kentucky and Missouri civic leaders resulted in Daniel's remains being reburied with grand ceremony on a bluff above the Kentucky state capitol at Frankfort. To this day, however, the argument over Daniel as "native son" has not been completely resolved. One expert recently determined that the bones Kentucky disinterred may not be Daniel's at all, and may in fact belong to a favorite slave buried at Rebecca's side.

No one will probably ever know for sure whether Daniel is resting in Kentucky. . .or Missouri. Not that it matters.

He was never known to stay put for very long.

Chronology

1681	William Penn receives charter for Pennsylvania.
1717	George Boone (Daniel Boone's grandfather) and his family settle near Philadelphia.
1734	*Daniel Boone is born.*
1750	Dr. Thomas Walker discovers the Cumberland Gap.
1754	The French and Indian War begins.
1755	*Daniel Boone escapes after Braddock's defeat at Fort Duquesne.*
1756	*Daniel Boone marries Rebecca Bryan.*
1763	The Treaty of Paris is signed, ending the French and Indian War. The Proclamation of 1763 forbids white settlement west of the Appalachian Mountains.
1765	The British Parliament passes the Stamp Act.
1767	*Daniel Boone reaches Kentucky for the first time.*
1769	*Daniel Boone, John Findley, and others explore Kentucky.*
1770	British soldiers fire into a Boston crowd, killing five men.
1773	*Daniel Boone leads settlers into Kentucky; the party is attacked before reaching the Cumberland Gap.* Colonists disguised as Indians dump British tea into Boston Harbor to protest the Tea Act.
1774	James Harrod establishes Harrodsburg, the first permanent white settlement in Kentucky.
1775	*Daniel Boone leads road cutters in clearing Wilderness Road for Henderson's settlers; Boonesborough is established.* Skirmishes at Lexington and Concord, Massachusetts, begin the Revolutionary War. Americans are defeated by the British in the Battle of Bunker Hill.

1776   The Declaration of Independence is signed.
        Kidnapped by Indians, Jemima Boone and Betsey and Fanny Callaway are rescued by Daniel Boone and other settlers.

1777   *Known in Kentucky as "the Year of the Three Sevens," a time of frequent Indian attacks.*
        The Americans win at Saratoga, New York, convincing the French to support their cause.

1777   Washington and his troops spend the winter of 1777-1778 at Valley Forge.

1778   *Daniel Boone and the salt makers are captured by the Shawnee.*
        Boonesborough survives a seven-day siege by the British and their Indian allies.
        Daniel Boone is court-martialed and acquitted.

1779   Clark secures the Northwest Territory for the Americans.

1780   The British defeat the Americans in the South, at Charleston and Camden, South Carolina.

1781   In the last major battle of the Revolutionary War, the British surrender at Yorktown.

1782   *The British and Indians attack Bryan's Station.*
        Daniel Boone and other Kentucky settlers are defeated by the British and Indians at the Battle of Blue Licks.

1783   The Treaty of Paris is signed between Great Britain and the Americans, recognizing the independence of the United States.

1788   The United States Constitution is ratified.

1789   George Washington is elected the first president of the United States; the first Congress meets in New York City.

1791   The Bill of Rights is ratified.

1792   Kentucky becomes a state.

1799   *Daniel Boone leads settlers to Missouri.*
        George Washington dies.

1800   *Daniel Boone is appointed syndic for the Femme Osage district.*

1803   President Thomas Jefferson purchases the Louisiana Territory.

1804   Lewis and Clark begin their expedition.

1812   American declares war against Britain.

1813   *Rebecca Boone dies.*

1815   *Daniel Boone travels to Kansas and Yellowstone country.*

1817   Work begins on the Erie Canal.

1820   *Daniel Boone dies.*

Bibliography

As I began tracking down reliable primary sources to write the biography of Daniel Boone, I faced some real challenges. Daniel was an uneducated man who never kept a diary or a journal and wrote few letters. Unfortunately, the most authentic version of his life story, which he had dictated to his son-in-law Flanders Callaway, fell into the Missouri River when a canoe capsized in 1814. The manuscript was never found.

One of my heroes in the search for the real Daniel Boone was Dr. Lyman C. Draper (1815–1891). Draper devoted fifty years, beginning in 1838, to the collection of letters, reminiscences, and stories from Boone's relatives, neighbors, and friends in Pennsylvania, North Carolina, Kentucky, Tennessee, and Missouri. Draper traveled by horseback to interview aging pioneers. He rescued crumbling family documents from attics, corncribs, and abandoned cabins. He spent a whole month with Nathan Boone to record what he remembered of his father. In the end, Draper assembled a staggering amount of information—most of it handwritten—filling nearly five hundred volumes. All of this material, plus the seven-hundred-page Boone biography he died before finishing, makes up the Draper Collection of the Wisconsin State Historical Society in Madison, Wisconsin. The microfilm record of Draper's work, which I used at the Newberry Library in Chicago, is nearly 12,300 feet from end to end.

Another early historian I found particularly helpful was John D. Shane (1812–1864). His work fills in rich detail about life on the frontier. Shane was a Kentuckian and a preacher who journeyed over back roads, recording stories told by Kentucky pioneers. Sixteen volumes of Shane's notes and four volumes of scrapbooks are now part of the Draper Collection. Other valuable letters and accounts by Boone family and friends were collected by Col. R. T. Durrett (1824–1913). His collection was stored in 269 boxes until it was finally bound and indexed. Today it is housed at the Joseph Regenstein Library, University of Chicago.

Local historians in Kentucky associated with the *Historical Quarterly* of The Filson Club of Louisville and the *Register* of the Kentucky State Historical Society in Frankfort have worked hard over the years to preserve and interpret maps, newspaper accounts, surveys, letters, diaries, and court records relating to Daniel Boone. Extensive notes and records housed at the office of the Yearly Meeting of the Religious Society of Friends, Philadelphia, provide important background information on the Boone family in Pennsylvania and in England. Official British military reports available through the Canadian Archives at Ottawa give the British side of the American Revolution, mention Daniel Boone directly in several instances, and describe the Indian situation in detail.

While not a complete listing, the books below also helped me write *Daniel Boone* and may provide useful further reading:

Arnow, Harriette S. *Seedtime on the Cumberland.* New York: Macmillan, 1960.

Bakeless, John. *Master of the Wilderness, Daniel Boone.* New York: William Morrow, 1939.

Bruce, H. Aldington. *Daniel Boone and the Wilderness Road.* New York: Macmillan, 1910.

Bryan, William S. and Rose, Robert. *A History of the Pioneer Families of Missouri.* St. Louis: Bryan Brand & Co., 1876.

Chidsey, Donal Barr. *The French and Indian War.* New York: Crown Publishers, 1969.

Clark, Thomas D. *Frontier America.* New York: Charles Scribner's Sons, 1969.

Day, John F. *Bloody Ground.* Lexington: University Press of Kentucky, 1981.

Dodderidge, Rev. Dr. Joseph. *Notes on the Settlement and Indian Wars of the Western Parts of Virginia and Pennsylvania.* 1824. Reprint. Albany: Joel Munsell, 1876.

Downes, Randolph C. *Council Fires on the Upper Ohio.* Pittsburgh: University of Pittsburgh Press, 1940.

Drake, Dr. Daniel. *Pioneer Life in Kentucky.* Edited by Dr. Emmet F. Horine. 1870. Reprint. New York: H. Schuman, 1948.

Durrett, Reuben T. *Bryant's Station.* Filson Club Publication No. 12. Louisville: John P. Morton & Co., 1897.

Elliott, Lawrence. *Daniel Boone, The Long Hunter.* London: George Allen & Unwin, 1977.

Federal Writers' Project, American Guide Series. *Hikes in Berks County, Pennsylvania.* Philadelphia: The William Penn Association, 1937.

Horowitz, David. *The First Frontier: The Indian Wars and America's Origins.* New York: Simon & Schuster, 1978.

Johnson, J. Stoddard. *First Explorations of Kentucky.* Filson Club Publication No. 13. Louisville: John P. Morton and Co., 1898.

Kelley, Joseph J., Jr. *Life and Times in Colonial Pennsylvania.* Harrisburg, Pa.: Stackpole Books, 1973.

Klein, Philip S. *A History of Pennsylvania.* University Park, Pa.: Pennsylvania State University Press, 1980.

Kopperman, Paul E. *Braddock at the Monongahela.* Pittsburgh: University of Pittsburgh Press, 1977.

Lagemann, Robert. *The Long Rifle.* New York: Eastern Acorn Press, 1980.

Lefler, Hugh Talmage. *North Carolina History Told by Contemporaries.* Chapel Hill: University of North Carolina Press, 1965.

Lofaro, Michael A. *The Life and Adventures of Daniel Boone.* Lexington: University Press of Kentucky, 1978.

Newman, Daisy. *A Procession of Friends: Quakers in America.* New York: Doubleday, 1972.

Peckham, Howard H. *The Colonial Wars.* Chicago: University of Chicago Press, 1964.

Pusey, William Allen. *The Wilderness Road to Kentucky.* New York: George H. Doran Co., 1921.

Ranck, George W. *Boonesborough.* Filson Club Publication No. 16. Louisville: John P. Morton & Co., 1901.

Rice, Otis, K. *Frontier Kentucky.* Lexington: University Press of Kentucky, 1975.

Rumple, Rev. Jethro. *A History of Rowan County, North Carolina.* Salisbury, N.C.: J. J. Bruner, 1881.

Speed, Thomas. *The Wilderness Road.* Filson Club Publication No. 2. Louisville: John P. Morton & Co., 1886.

Spraker, Hazel Atterbury. *The Boone Family.* Rutland, Vt.: Tuttle Co., 1922.

West, Jessamyn. *The Quaker Reader.* New York: Viking Press, 1962.

Young, Chester. *Westward into Kentucky: Narrative of Daniel Trabue.* Lexington: University Press of Kentucky, 1981.

Index

Numbers in italics refer to pages in the photo insert, which appears between pages 80 and 81 of the text.

MOUNT VERNON CHRISTIAN SCHOOL
820 Blackburn Road   Ph: 424-9152
Mount Vernon, Washington 98273